COURSES AND WORKSHOPS

Teaching earns money!

Graeme Smith

PUBLISHED ON AMAZON.com
by
LABYRINTH BOOKS

DEDICATION:

This book is dedicated to my family.
    Hele-ly (Ly).
    my wife:

    Ingrid.
    our daughter:

    Marie.
    my former wife:

    Fiona, Natalie and Michael
    our children:

    Georgie
    Michael's wife:

    Pearl, Kiki and Martha.
    their children:

They have put up with me for many years and I thank them for that.

I hope this book gives an idea into what occupied me much of the time.

They have all achieved worthwhile and interesting careers.

In the absence of much help from me.

I congratulate them for their achievements.

THANKS:

I greatly appreciate the contribution made to this book by comments and suggestions from:

Mike Barr – Adelaide, Australia

Richard Bruland - Los Angeles, USA

Tracey Creighton - Merimbula, Australia

Evelyn Dunphy – Maine, USA

Geoff Fellows – Wagga Wagga, Australia

Michelle Grace - Brisbane, Australia

Leanne Halls – North Sydney, Australia

Heidi Jeffries – Ferny Hills, Australia

Kathy Kay Voysey - Mudgee, Australia.

Vince Miller – publisher:

       ('Australian Artist' and 'International Artist)

John Newell - Ontario, Canada

David Voigt – Yarramalong, Australia.

HOW TO USE THIS BOOK.

First think - then do.
Usually people don't think through things to the level they need to.
Because of that, they have projects instead of tasks on their "to do" list.
Leading to procrastination as it's not been broken down to a task level.

So go through your book once to understand it.
Go through it again.

Then start at the idea you would like to implement first.
Make notes of the steps you'll need to take and the resources required.
Use the notes to create a step by step system to implement the guide.
Often you'll not refer back to an original, as you created YOUR system.

The first question you ask and answer is "Why is this being done?"
How does this align with where you want to get to?
What are the strategic implications of doing this?
Does this fit with getting to a goal in the shortest and fastest time?

What would it be like if it were totally successful?
Define it - what is success for this project and how will you know?

Now brainstorm all the tasks that are involved in your project.
It's important not to go linear too fast with this.
By linear, I mean step one, step two, step three, and step four.
You end up cutting off options.
Plan step 1, 2, and 3, a specific step that might be number four.
If you start steps quickly, other ways of 1, 2 or 3 may not appear.

The first third of any brainstorming session is really easy.
Just come up with lots of ideas.
The second third is challenging - go through ideas see where they lead.
Then push yourself to think a little bit outside the box.
That's often where the big idea is!

That's where the best way to get a project done fastest - is.
Most people never get to that level and short-change themselves.
Then their project takes longer and they also procrastinate.
This final brainstorming part of the equation is incredibly important.

Once you fully brainstorm put your options into a linear sequence.
Then you can figure out what you've overlooked.
Everything becomes obvious as you get your tasks in order.
Add missing steps and you have laid out your task list for this project.

Once you've organized the tasks into a linear process decide:
What things can you start immediately?
What can be started that doesn't depend on things to occur before?
Obviously that is step one.
Step 5 or 6 or 20 that don't really rely on anything else to get done.
You can get started on them right away too.

Now use a folder.
Write things you think of at the time and also cross off things as done
Add in stuff that is relevant from time to time.

WHAT IS MARKETING?

Marketing is the process of finding buyers AND making sales
It is exactly the same process no matter what is being sold!
Sometimes the process is simple like selling apples at a roadside stall.

In other cases it is very complex.
Selling aero-planes to a government's air-force is an example of that.
Most, including selling artworks, is somewhere in between these poles.

Think about fishing and you'll understand marketing.
Does a fisherman catch anything out in a desert?
NO, for there are simply no fish there.

You must market where there are possible buyers.
A fisherman must go where the fish are – where there is water.
That's a start but there are still no fish in a swimming pool are there?
They need to be in the right kind of water – a river, lake or at sea.

But different fish swim in different waters!
Sharks and marlin are in the ocean, while bream live mainly in rivers.
Likewise you must know who you are targeting with your marketing.
Will it be businesses, first home buyers, investors or what?
Each will need a different marketing program.

OK you are now in the right water for the kind of fish you are after!
Are you there at the right time?

Some species are nocturnal and are not caught during the day.
So your marketing needs to be when the target is most receptive.
Will it be at work, nights or weekends?

You're at the right place and time, what do you use to catch fish?
Usually you'll have a fishing rod.
Is it the right kind for the fish you want to catch?

You won't catch a shark with the kind of rod that takes a trout!
Your marketing must be attractive to the people you are after.

Do you have the right bait?
Again different bait attracts different fish.
A carcass for the shark but just a worm for many other species.
Can you provide something that your target market will find attractive?

But throwing any bait into the water catches nothing at all!
The bait must be attached to a hook.
Without the fish taking the hook there is no catch.
Different hooks are needed for different kinds of fish.

Different hooks are also needed for different markets.
The hook that will get your market to take the next step towards a
purchase is the right hook.
But this only needs to be a little step.

But hooks only catch the fish.
They're in the water, not your boat or beach so attach the hook to a line.
What is your line like?
Is it strong enough you the fish you are after?
Again this varies for the kind of fish.

How do you get a prospect to seriously consider what you have?
For someone buying a print it will not need to be sophisticated.
But selling an original Renoir will be considerably more complicated.

That doesn't bring in a fish the line needs a reel for that to happen.
Again different reels for different fish.
The right reel allows you to bring the fish to the end of your fishing line.
But it's still not in the boat is it?

You need to lift the fish out of the water to your boat or on a beach.
Fishing nets do this.

But now you have your catch.
The fish is yours to do what you want with.

You can even sell the fish!
But who might want to buy?
It could be someone sells the fish as food or live for a fish-tank or pool.
They could even be for re-stocking natural water places.

Where can you find them?
You must look where the fish buyers are!
Follow the path of the fisherman.
And eventually you have a prospect asking can they buy.
You have made a sale **AND** you can make more sales the same way.

OK how do you make the sale?
There are five key groups.
So it's a five step process.

In order you work from the top through to the bottom group.
SUSPECTS are people who might possibly want what you sell.
PROSPECTS are people likely to want what you have for sale.
BUYERS are those who have bought what you are selling.
REPEAT BUYERS continue to buy what you sell.
ADVOCATES help you sell to others.

The reverse sequence is the order of importance to your sales.

INDEX: SUCCESSFUL COURSES.

Acknowledgement:
John Hill, West Sussex, United Kingdom assisted with proof reading.
Many of his comments were incorporated in this book.
I am very grateful to John for his help.
John and Sakura's website is www.johnhillwatercolour.com

Chapter One: Your career vision.

1. Teaching is part of the business of art
2. What is your 'X' factor?
3. Can it be done?
4. You can gain knowledge in various ways.

1. Teaching is a commercial option for an artist.

This can be in addition to painting and other artistic activity.
There are many people specializng in helping people understand art.
You can choose whether to become involved in teaching or not.
If you're in business then business principles apply to your activities.
Musicians, poets, salespeople, accountants, hairdressers are the same.

John Hill (UK) - It's hard to paint and teach with no compromise.
John says successful teaching requires creativity and hard work.
Often this can be to the detriment of the teacher's own art.
Students influence technique, style, palette, subject matter of teacher.
Some established artists teach, based on their personal painting skills.

Whether to specialize or not, is a choice artists have.
Teachers can do the same but you can't specialize and not specialize.
The beginning artist tends to try all ideas, media, subjects and so forth.
A beginning teacher often does this too!
They have to do this to find out what they like best.

Some artists even do this for a very long period.
They become life-long students and there's nothing wrong with that!
But many discover that certain things interest them more than others.

Maybe it's various combinations of media, colours, or subjects.
They follow this interest and there's nothing wrong with that either.

Teachers can do the same.
Because of their focus, they get better at their specialty.
They apply knowledge and experience with depth and understanding.
Business is not prejudiced towards, or against, any particular sort of art.
Realist, facile, studious, contemporary, all can be a professional career.
That could be as an artist, teacher or both.

Sound commercial orientation is complementary to artistic activity.
An artist who has a need to create, a need to sell and a need to teach.
Can do all of them, without compromising any of them.
Yes it's possible but due to time constraints it may not be easy.

2. What is your 'X' factor?

A consultant was brought into a billion dollar atomic power plant.
A technical problem that reduced the efficiency of the entire operation.
The plant's engineers were unsuccessful in identifying the problem.
So they couldn't find a solution either.

2 days careful study of many dials and gauges in the control room.
The consultant climbed a ladder and made a large black 'X' on a gauge.
When this equipment was replaced, the plant returned to full capacity.
A few days later the plant supervisor got an invoice for $100,000.

The consultant was questioned about the size of the account.
It seemed excessive based on the work performed.
"Standing around for a few days and marking a black 'X' on a gauge".
The consultant's response was to itemize his invoice like this:
Placing 'X' on gauge: $ 1.00 and knowing which gauge: $ 99.999.00
Total: $100,000.00

This principle applies in everyday life as well.
The 'X' in life represents where to focus your attention, time and energy.
This 'X' is your Focal Point.
What you do, at any time to get the best result in a specific area of life.

An area often neglected by artists and artist teachers.
A valuable Focal Point 'X' in the financial area is your "hourly rate."
Once adopted it's crucial to go to the next level of professional career.
Simply stated, your hourly rate is your annual income divided by 2,000.
If you are earning $100,000 per year, your hurly rate is $50 per hour.

It is the key to the proper allocation of your time and energy.
A simple way to assess if you should do any particular task is to ask:
Would I pay someone $50 per hour (or your hourly rate) to do this task?
If the answer is no, then it is not the financially best use of your time.
You should either eliminate the task, or delegate it to a suitable person.

That person earns their appropriate hourly rate.
If your goal is to earn, say, $200,000 per year.
Don't spend time or energy on tasks worth less than $100 an hour.
If you do, you cannot make your target - it's that simple!

Wwhat is your current hourly rate and what is your 12-month goal?
Do you spend time daily on tasks you wouldn't pay your hourly rate for?
If not, congratulations, you are well on your way to achieving your goal.
Which tasks do you eliminate and which will you delegate and to whom?
Such choices are key deciders of the probability of reaching your goal.

How much do you want to earn in the next year?
Then calculate your hourly rate and apply it.

3. Can it be done?

Can what can be done, you might reasonably ask.
Can you can make a living from art is the answer.
Not just a living, but **VERY** good living as some artists do.
Most don't.
But it's not the art that makes the difference, but the attitude.
Same goes for making a really good living from teaching art.

Recently I was reading an old car magazine (one of my interests).
I came across a story that I thought might appeal to you.
The story on Alistair Brookham (p70 - 72, 'Sports Driver', issue 6 1990).

Alistair makes model cars for a living!
In fact he makes model racing and sports cars, not just any car
Before he started he raced cars, and a mechanical draftsman too.
In addition his father was a model-maker, although not professionally.
So he did have a good background.

He knew workmanship, enthusiasm and dedication are important.
But he made decisions before embarking on a model-making career.
He had to decide which car to build (yes which one).
He also had to consider where he could find buyers.
How much they were prepared to pay (not what he wanted –not then).
Back in **1982** he started building two models.
They were Ferrari racing cars because he was sure there'd be interest.

Before picking up any tools, he did a huge amount of research.
He studied books and all available drawings and photographs.
He has a large library these days.
Following exhaustive research Alistair relies on his drafting background,
He draws every component to the exact size that he will make them.
This is not easy as he is mainly working from photographs.
They may not show accurate measurements due to distortion.
Sometimes he has to make a part several times before he gets it right!

Alistair spends about two months on the design aspect.
He draws each part in the order he will assemble them.
He works from seven in the morning until around nine at night.
These days he usually builds five cars a year!
Alistair's estimate is that it takes him 800 hours to build a model.

He worked part time on those first two Ferraris, for three months.
However it became obvious that he would have to make it full time.
His modelling career depended on the success of those first two cars.
They were sold, but there were no repeat sales or even enquiries.
So it was back to the drafting board for Alastair.

In (1986) an English sports car magazine ran an article on his cars.
Subsequent interest set the ball rolling again and demand was great.
When I read the article, he had enough work for the next ten years.
He asks for a considerable deposit and expects cash prior to delivery.
His clients range from museums to investors and enthusiasts.
One thing they all have in common is an ability to pay a price tag.
This relates to the time, effort and skill that has gone into the car.

There's a message here for you whether as an artist or teacher.
The better background you have the greater your chance of success.
But even with this you still need a professional attitude.

Right from the start Alastair was focused on his potential clients.
He didn't leave sales to chance.
He does a great deal of research before starting.
How much research do you do?
What about for your teaching?

Most artists toss off a work and expect people will pay for it.
The expectation is people will pay because an artist produced the work.
That's even though it was done to meet their own creative needs.
This attitude is truly amateurish and doesn't deserve encouragement.

4. You can gain knowledge in various ways.

Until you acquire experience acting on that you won't move ahead.
One way is to teach that knowledge to others.
There is a misconception surrounding the concept of knowledge.
You've probably heard the phrase: "Knowledge is power."
BUT this relationship is not necessarily correct!

Knowledge is NOT power.
Knowledge is linked to something but only some knowledge to power.
Then it's about how to exercise power, obtain it, or use it in another way.
That knowledge is power but it also depends what power is too.

There are many people who are highly educated (have knowledge).
But some of them are also penniless (not powerful).
As you read this there's someone sunbathing on his or her own yacht.
They thank themselves for dropping out of high school.
Yes there are successful dropouts (even some artists).

In physics, a fundamental lesson concerns itself with power.
Power is defined as the rate at which energy is converted.
The lesson then defines two forms of energy:

Potential Energy
The energy stored in a system -- like your mind or body.

Kinetic Energy
The energy driven by action

In physics, potential energy isn't power; it's just potential power.
The true form of power that everyone seeks is "Kinetic" power.
The word "kinetic" stems from the Greek word kinesis, which is motion.
So true power (kinetic energy) is driven by action or application.

So knowledge is usually "potential energy" (or "potential power").
When buying a book many artists buy a program and don't apply it.
They think having "potential power" (book), means success as an artist.
Even reading a book is still potential power and thus potential success.

They internally tell themselves,
"If I buy this book, I'll succeed in my professional career.
I'll know what to do to be a successful professional artist.
I'll make money, my wife will be proud, and can quit my boring job."
A few months down the track they find that nothing has changed.

They continue on looking for some other "potential power."
They buy another book, or move to other potential sources of success.
It's a vicious cycle resulting in a life of wasted effort and disappointment.
This cycle is one that can be easily avoided, and I can help you avoid.

People can go through their life buying "potential power,"
They become let down, and repeat the cycle over and over.
Potential power might be a college degree, masters' program or course,
Potential power alone will not result in success.

Success and physics share the same formula:
$(P)*(A) = K$, which leads to Success
P = Potential Energy
A = Application
K = Kinetic Energy

Here it is again but with alternative data:
$(P)*(A) = K$, which leads to Success
P = Book
A = Actually do stuff
K = Follow a path to success as a professional artist

Yet not all those who succeed as professional artist require P.
So what's the secret to succeeding – just one letter: A

In the formula above, A stands for Application.
The difference between artists who succeed and fail is application.
Apply Potential Energy with Action and find professional success.

Whether you get a book or not is entirely up to you.
If you don't have the time to do anything then don't buy.
BUT please don't just "buy" a book, instead "apply" the book you buy.

If you are a professional money is a measure of how well you do.
It's not the motivation for that's your desire to follow your dream.
But it does say something about how well you've followed the dream.
It also makes achieving your dream more feasible.

Teaching what you know can earn regular and substantial income.
What you know can be based on your personal experience.
It can also be based on the experience of other knowledgeable people.
Use what they have written as a curriculum for your teaching.
Use this strategy properly and you can make a full time living.
What have you actually done as a result?

Chapter Two: How do people learn?

1. **How do you obtain knowledge?**
2. **How do people think?**
3. **Teaching the mental aspects!**
4. **How a young artist developed his artistic ability.**
5. **How do students improve their painting?**

1. How do you obtain knowledge?

There is little to be gained by JUST READING what anyone writes.
To get **ANY** benefit you must actually **DO** something!
AND the speed of your progress is likely to vary.
Depending on where you live, work you do and your single-mindedness.

For example how do you learn from any book?
Initially you get familiar with the language and culture in the book.
You experiment tentatively and cautiously, just a few ideas or strategies.
Probably some things did **NOT** give the hoped for results.
BUT others provided a pleasant surprise.

You went from reading to doing and NOW learning.
You got serious about implementing ideas from the book you bought.
Not all of them naturally but an increasing amount.

You highlighted things to DO and ACT on.
That means you wrote them down so the ideas were not forgotten.
Favourable results and you are more enthusiastic about the opportunity.
You start to re-invent your professional career from top to bottom.

That's when the profound breakthroughs commence.
Others were also excited as you shared discoveries and achievements.
You are reason and commonsense.
Iin an art-world of myths that don't work!

Increased confidence means you have an entirely new mind-set.
You're ready for new opportunities, and willing to try new approaches.
You have a better career as well.
Family, friends, even the skeptics when you began using the book.
Now admire your success and are amazed at your career growth.
Friends, artist peers, even those who're envious, start asking for advice.
Probably you could even run a course from the book?

"So I've been busy promoting myself like crazy and it's starting to work …. I find it all fascinating and fun and I love the anticipation of where it might lead." (Lesley White - Prince George, Canada)

2. How do people think?

I once read a report about golfers (not artists).
Most successful professional golfers say the game is 95% mental.
Lesser golfers find this hard to believe.
They pay professionals to teach how to hit a ball, and stand properly.

It's the same in our field isn't it?
Many artists also believe technical mastery must be acquired first.

The report was about research done at the University of Chicago.
Professional and amateur golfers were compared.
The brain activation of the two golfing groups was studied.
Some areas were highly active in amateurs but silent for professionals.

These areas were related to motor planning and execution.
An area that co-ordinates sensory input with emotions was studied.
Also cognition, movement co-ordination and voluntary movement.
Both were highly active in the amateurs but not the professionals.

Because the amateurs were taking too long and unable to focus.
It's likely they were more anxious about their shot than the professional.
Too much data inhibits motor planning and performance.
Thus activating these areas of the brain.

The amateur is thinking that each shot is a new shot.
A professional knows they're the same as before, already internalized.
Their game is mental for they don't need to focus on physical aspects.
The amateur has to consciously consider each shot.
This is consistent with learned skills (the authors do not say this).

Professional golfers skills are such, they don't need to focus there.
There is little or no relevant brain activity for the actions are automatic.
They focus on other areas, like pin placement, slope of the green etc.

But the amateur has too much to focus on and think about.
That means they do not have time for the mental aspect of the game.

You'll understand this better if I relate it to driving a car.
When you learn to drive, everything has to be explained.
You think through the process of driving almost in words.
I'd better brake here, turn the indicator, now, and so on.

Eventually your skill improves and you become a better driver.
Now you don't need to talk your way through each step of driving.
You just do it.

The better you get, the less you think (well consciously anyway).
AND the faster you can respond to whatever circumstances that arise.
Just imagine you have to actually talk your way through an intersection?
You'd have an accident for sure – just about every time!

Talking is too slow so it's an inefficient method for guiding actions.
But you don't drive without any thought, or you'd still have accidents.
When people become skilled drivers they internalize their thinking.

What happens is their thinking has become non-verbal
This is faster and more efficient than language thinking

In many sports things happen very quickly there is the evidence.
The top batsman hooks the fast bowler to the fence.
A soccer player angles the ball past a keeper to the top of the net.

None of these actions is accidental or unintended.
Yet the player couldn't think it through in words in time to do the action.
When you drive the car it's exactly the same.
AND in golf it's the same too.
In fact learning and applying **ANY** skill happens this way.

Think about a child learning to walk.
The child just does it, without concern for what might happen.
The child is unaware of the consequences of failure and thus unworried.
The pro golfer is also unworried and thus confident.

What would happen if golfers were first taught mental aspects?
That's instead of the skills?

Would they learn the skills anyway?
Would they just do it!
Would they become better golfers?

The archer hits the target, partly by pulling and partly by letting go.
I remember reading this many years ago (and I can't remember where).
The professional has learnt the art of letting go.
It comes with experience, skill and confidence.

What about art students?
Do they think everything out, step by step, before painting anything?
This is the amateur golfer way.
Confidence is the key – they should just do it!

Then their style will emerge from what they do.
Exhibitions where works look the same or similar show the artist's style.
You may like it or not, but it's there (e.g. van Gogh).

Skill comes from practice, style comes from within.
Exhibitions that look like several different artists painted the works.
Lack style but possibly have a mastery of skill if it just one artist's works.

3. Teaching the mental aspects!

Students should just do it without concern for what might happen.
Do not worry about the consequences of failure.
Paint quickly.
Paint small.
Re-work many.

Make sure all materials are available to allocate to the student.
For example start with a small paper rectangle, a brush, and red paint,
Later use white paint.
Then later still several thin strips of white paper.
Eventually use some blue paint.

It doesn't matter what they do at the start.
Anything will do.
As long as they do something.

That's really the first task – to start!
Next task is to develop whatever was done.
The student's mind only needs a few marks to feed on.

Use extra material only if finished using those previously provided.
This will be when the student stops working.
Do not be in a hurry to provide more stuff
Keep the quantities small too.

Conclude what they have done so far.
Just do not issue any more stuff.

OK what did you notice?

4. How a young artist developed his artistic ability.

I tested an art education program in a primary (elementary) school.
Teaching was closely linked to the materials issued to the pupils.
The particular material combinations chosen were not random.
They were to introduce quite specific experiences to the pupils.
The challenge was to see what they'd create with a given combination.
This often, but not always, included paint (like the previous exercise).

One teacher noticed a particular boy over a series of lessons.
In the earliest lessons there were always two blobs present in the work.
It did not matter what he was given out by the teacher.
Over a period of time these blobs gradually changed into two birds.
They were just basic symbol-type birds, such as most people might do.
As the lessons continued the birds improved.
There were more details and eventually recognizable as budgerigars.

It became a challenge for the teacher.
He realized the boy made budgerigars no matter what materials issued.
He tried to find a combination of materials that couldn't be budgerigars.
He always made birds, even pin-pricked budgerigars on paper.
Could this kid might become the best budgerigar artist in the world?
If he continued, I'd say every chance.
He was becoming a creative thinker which is what the teacher wanted.

Why did he do this?
Well the teacher discovered (surprise) he had two pet budgerigars.
They meant more to the boy than anything else.
His art gave him an opportunity to express his feelings and knowledge.
That's because the teacher **DIDN'T** tell him what to do,

This story shows the benefit of focus.
Artists who focus on painting what is important benefit in a similar way.
Paint because there's something you want to do or an idea to develop.
Anything intrinsic to the work and their experience is all that's needed.

Let's say a student wanted to learn to paint the human figure?
Then they paint figures **BUT** do **NOT** worry about how they turn out.
Just paint them and in time they'll improve just like the birds did!
Just do them.
They improve if the motivation is strong enough **AND** you do enough!
It's also how they can develop confidence!

They could learn to paint snow leopards using this approach.
Start by copying photographs.
Gradually experiment by manipulating the images of the snow leopards.
Eventually they'll paint believable snow leopards from memory!
I know an artist who learned to paint polar bears using this approach!

5. How do students improve their painting?

Style emerges from what is done.
If the student is a passionate and individual.
Then anything they do, including painting, will have those qualities.
So do not worry about such matters for they look after themselves.

Maintaining motivation and enthusiasm is linked to why they paint.
It's my belief that artists paint because there is a challenge.
Can I make a painting of this subject?
What will happen if I use those colours?
How will this look but in that medium etc.?

If there is no challenge, then there is no reason for painting.
It's an exercise and tends to become repetitious and eventually boring.
A lot of art lessons are like this!

A commission is just a particular kind of challenge.
Explore variations, say of subjects, styles, colours, or whatever needed.
There's no pressure to do this, but no reason not to either.
One painting often leads to the next, and even five or six variations.

Chapter Three: Your career plan.

1. The 100 hour rule for taking the plunge!

2. How do galleries sell?

3. Can you run your own gallery?

4. What kind of gallery do you want?

1. The 100 hour rule for taking the plunge!

Paintings are WHAT you do and a GALLERY is where you sell.
"The 100 Hour Rule" can start your own gallery to a consistent income.

Do 100 hours of REAL work focused on ONE outcome.
Break that down to 10 hours a week for 10 weeks, under 3 months.
That's a **FIRST** step to full-time gallery success - part-time success.

BUT the 100 hours IS ADDITIONAL to time organising the gallery.
There are two key parts.
100 hours of **REAL** work.
Focused on **ONE** outcome.

Follow up with the "500 Hour Rule".
500 hours of **REAL** work focused on **ONE** outcome.
Will give you a gallery so you make a full-time income.
You have no regular job to go to and the hassles attached to that gone!
At 10 hours a week, less than 1 year and you have your own gallery.

It's a rule to move from "professional artist" to "artist with gallery"!
Imagine this time next year you've **DONE IT**.
You now have your own gallery and it's a great feeling, isn't it?

BUT you've worked 10 hours a week and that hasn't happened yet!
When I started I had to figure out what didn't work to find what does.
I'm sure you're experiencing the same.
That why it takes most artists a whole lot longer than I've suggested.

You do what you think is best.
For in the past no-one showed the best way.
My goal, is sharing what **REALLY** works instead of what **DOESN'T.**

Its human nature to look for "greener pastures over the fence"!
I've been guilty of this just like you.
Something new comes out and marketing hits psychological triggers.
Next thing you know, hours, days, even weeks have passed.
But you are in the same place you were when you started.

Instead stay focused on one outcome and the steps to success.
Only look for things that make that career goal more successful faster.
NOT a distraction from your outcome.

How can you tell if you do "REAL Work" or "Busy Work"?
Here are some examples of busy work:
Reading an inbox full of 539 emails just because they are there.
Buying an eBook, skimming through it, and then never doing anything.
Watching more free online videos somebody posted.
Dabbling, doing a little here, a little there, with no plan.
No plan on where you are going, or steps to complete to get there

Is this typical of how you work on your career?
Turn on computer, download email, read the latest emails?
Clicking on a few links, watching a video for 30 minutes.
Going back to emails to see what new messages you need to read.
Checking out your favourite site as you deserve a break from work.
Think about a new blog post you could write but don't write the thoughts.
Open your website account to see how many new subscribers you got.
But you are disappointed again that the same 23 people on your list.
Download more emails and spend 45 minutes reading and clicking.
It's getting late, so close after a productive day working on your career.

During that entire time
There was not a single action taken that moved your gallery forward.

Nothing that made your gallery better today than the day before.
There was a lot of time spent on activity, but no time spent on action.

Here's the million dollar question to ask yourself:
If you spent 10 hours a week that moved your gallery plans forward.
How great would your success become over the next few months?
You run rings around the person who spends time doing "busy work".

2. You should make money from your gallery.

Making money from your gallery is honourable and worthwhile.
I strongly reject the notion receiving money will diminish your integrity.

Your income is the ONLY objective way to measure your success.
Reputation, grants, fame, in the art establishment, can't be measured.
So I do not concern myself with them.

What about me - am I an artist?
Yes I do paint, and have had many one man exhibitions.
Originally I was a primary (elementary) school teacher.
Then I studied art at the National Art School (Sydney).
I received distinctions in every subject in my final year.
This led to being an art consultant with the NSW Education Department.
I wrote books on art teaching and art educational programs.

I opened an art gallery, with no business background.
I also started exhibiting other artist's work and I was lucky, I survived.
I know many artists, some well-known in Australia and others starting.
I am friends with collectors and have an insight into their art world view.

I also commenced and ran a picture framing business.
In addition I was a consultant curator at Charles Sturt University.

Along with my wife, I've been a business coach.
So have an understanding and association with mainstream business/
That knowledge allows me to draw comparisons with our own industry.
I learnt a many things that provide a basis for articles I write these days.
I read regularly, looking for new, different and better ways to do things.

Not long ago I was interviewed by Paul Buckingham.
Paul runs a business here in Australia, called The Mentor Club.
He puts out a CD each month which contains an interview he has done.
They are usually with a prominent business person about their business.

They are short interviews he feels his subscribers are interested in.
I was one of the support acts.

I have a broader range of experience than most in the art business.
I've not mentioned my background in sport, and with car clubs.
Passed over is much of my educational consultancy and gallery years.
Each of these has contributed in various ways to what I do now.
I've started new ventures, developed them, and had new challenges.
Sometimes I have also revisited earlier projects, or elements of projects.
I do not hold myself up as outstandingly successful though.
But you can learn what I learned.

3. How do galleries sell?

A visitor to my home saw a painting that he really liked.
He asked how much it was so I named a figure and a sale was made.
What he actually bought was my palette that I then signed and framed.
Would you do that in your gallery?

Galleries basically sell artworks, most often paintings.
If they do not sell they go out of business.
Even if they sell they still go out of business, if sales aren't profitable.
So you can see a gallery is just like any other regular business.
You should not think of yours in any other way.

A gallery doesn't exist so an artist has a place to show work.
A gallery exhibits the work of an artist because it's a proven way to sell.
This applies to you in your own gallery as well.
You must believe sales can be made, either now or in the medium term.

There are three ways a business that sells, can acquire stock.
Manufacture it themselves.
Purchase it from a manufacturer.
Hold the work on consignment, paying the manufacturer after the sale.

You are the manufacturer of your own artworks.
It follows that you can sell them yourself.
This could be retail level, direct to the client (from your studio or gallery).
You can sell wholesale to someone who then sells at a retail level.

So perhaps you could be a wholesaler?
Wholesale price must be less than retail or a retailer can't make money.
Unless they sell at a higher price than other people (like you).
The retailer also bears the risk (large for artworks) the work will not sell.
In slow moving retail areas mark-up's are high to compensate for this.
Quick selling lines (food) may have a mark-up of a few percent.
Jewellery can be 150% or even more.

To sell direct to a gallery, your price must be so they make money.
The amount made compensate for other works that haven't sold.
If you paint very quickly you can consider this approach.

You may have work on consignment and then be paid after a sale.
This eliminates risk tor for a gallery, but you bear the cost of no sales.
Due to slow moving nature of art sales (more works than buyers to buy).
Consignment selling is common, as in real estate for the same reasons.
But even here the retail seller still has to make money.
The amount earned from a sale on consignment is called a commission.
No commission is earned unless there is a sale.

To consign to a gallery, your price must be so they make money.
When they sell to the client.

Joe Bloggs (an artist) sells from his studio gallery.
The price for each work varies but let's call it $A for artist's price.
Sold on consignment the wholesale price paid to an artist should be:
$A − c (commission).
If a gallery or dealer buys to resell the wholesale price should be:
$A − c − rf (risk factor).

Joe has a work, which he sells for $1000.
When sold on consignment Joe gets $600 (- $400 or 40% commission).
If he sells wholesale (not easy) Joe gets $300 or what he can negotiate.
These sorts of figures are the reality of the art business world.

Space in normal galleries is limited.
There are regular exhibitors and only have one or two new artists a year.
This even was the case when I ran a gallery.

The 'do-it-yourself' option for most artists is really the only choice.
It's the alternative to waiting to be discovered, which takes a long time.
Often artist's galleries occupy otherwise vacant shop-fronts.
Warehouses, commercial basements, home living rooms, garages too.

Such galleries, where they exist are a vital part in a local art scene.
Frequently they are set up by recent graduates of an art course.
Others decide they must take the plunge or nothing will happen for them.
Often a belief it's public exposure unhindered by commercial constraints.

Running your own gallery is not for the faint hearted.
They are time consuming, financially demanding and very risky.
Even low rental can be too high for an artist with few sales, or none.
If you share with other artists the costs can be reduced.
But decision making becomes considerably more complicated.
Often it is a loose working arrangement between several people.

Running your own gallery could be a stepping stone though.
It could be to obtain proper representation in commercial galleries.
Then you better understand how a commercial gallery operates.
Also why they do things how they do.
But it's a pretty hard way to find that out!
You are more realistic about the commercial realities of your own work.
Commercial gallery people visit artist run galleries, to discover artists!

So ideally if you can be situated near other galleries, it's best.
BUT that is only if the financial aspects are right.
Be financially cautious, as most artist run galleries have short
existences.

4. What kind of gallery do you want?

Space in galleries is limited so many artists have their own gallery.
The "do-it-yourself" option for most artists is really the only choice.
A gallery will allow greater profit margins than selling at someone else's.
Although it will be more time consuming and costly.

BUT I want to introduce a different approach for you to think about.
The **MARKET** oriented gallery as opposed to **VIEWER** oriented gallery.
The difference is similar to that of a car dealership and a car museum.

The viewer oriented gallery is emphasizes viewing the artworks.
Special care is given to lighting, how the works are hung, and so on.
The emphasis is on the works and their presentation.
National, State and regional Galleries are all set up this way.
In fact most galleries are set up and operate using this philosophy.

Many people who visit galleries are lookers.
This is not too surprising, for that's how we enjoy art isn't it?
If they've no intention of buying, in the motor-trade they're "tyre-kickers".
They don't waste time on tyre-kickers as there's no commission.
Wouldn't it be best if **ONLY** buyers, or potential buyers, came in?

A market oriented gallery is set up to sell artworks.
Anything done is to help sell the works, whether on display or not.
It is hard to tell the difference between the two if you are a viewer.
A possible difference could be labels attached to, or near, each work.
In a viewer-oriented gallery they are usually very informative.
Title, media, measurement, date artist's name is usually provided.
There may be a price and biographical or critical information as well.

The market oriented gallery may have no label, or merely a title.
A visitor has to seek information provided in a viewer oriented gallery.
So the visitor is engaged in a conversation with the sales person!

Lack of information helps a sales person identify potential buyers.
Excess information, potential buyers are anonymous.
Except if they buy.
The opportunity to turn potential buyers into actual buyers is lost.

Do you want to make your gallery a more efficient way to sell?
Do you still do things that are carry-over from viewer-oriented gallery?
Probably when you are open anybody can come in.
What's wrong with that you might say?
It's an inefficient use of **YOUR** time to wait in case someone comes in.

Chapter Four: Making it work.
1. Think outside the square!
2. With a market oriented gallery the focus is on sales.
3. Would a stand-by system work?
4. Making the most of your time!
5. Time management gets things done!

1. Think outside the square!

You've probably heard of 'thinking outside the square'?
It's a nice pat thing that people say.

I write on the assumption that most readers are painters.
But I have had one or two potters, subscribe to the newsletter I write.
These potters are looking for new ideas.
They could get information from within potting circles.
But there's more chance of a breakthrough if a search is elsewhere.
That's thinking outside the square.
But to get something really useful they need to translate what is written.
So it becomes something that suits their own situation.
All translate what they read to something useful or nothing happens.

I remember reading, quite a long time ago, about Picasso.
He decided that he'd like to work with clay and sought out some potters.
All were keen to show what to do and demonstrate various techniques.
Picasso would have none of this.
He shut himself in a shed for a week and then re-appeared.
The potters were amazed he developed new ways of working with clay.
They could only have come about through Picasso's unique vision.

He did not want to be side-tracked by working in the way of others.
Before he'd had a chance to develop his own approach.
He was really stepping outside the (ceramic) square.
Picasso's discoveries would have been unlikely had this not been done.

Let's stay with the potting idea a bit more.
Clay can be turned on a wheel so it's possible to make similar pieces.
Selling similar pieces is a common marketing problem for potters.
But not usually for painters although reproduction prints are a parallel.

Potters produce two lines, production pieces and one-off works.
Production pieces are utilitarian, mugs, cups, saucers, jugs and the like.
They're "bread and butter" for the potter, and most time is spent on this.
Because many are the same, they make them quickly in large quantities.
This is of course essential as they're mostly sold for quite low prices.

The more creative work is the artistic output of the potter.
They use less total time but each gets more than a production piece.
These "one-off" items are also more highly priced.
Some potters are sought after for their artistic work and sell in galleries.

In my gallery-owing day, I promoted painters, but had a potter.
In my gallery the one-off works easily outsold production pieces.
We only sold a few of the production pieces, which were always cheap.
With one potter, my experience is limited and may not apply elsewhere.

A potter should have different outlets for different kinds of work.
Production pieces at places where there was a likelihood of many sales.
Tourist resorts, shopping centres and markets where many people are.
The one-off pieces at prestige locations.
Here exclusiveness, status and higher price more likely.
Perhaps potters do this?

But artists can do the same as well!
Production artworks and your own creative works, just like the potter.

There are well-known and successful artists who've done this.
In some circles they're looked down on but they laugh going to a bank.

I met a young printmaker, whom I hadn't seen for several years.
His work is technically superb.

The images very complex and highly charged with symbolism.
He is very serious about his art and "making it" critically.
In fact he has already achieved quite a deal in this regard.
So I naturally asked him how his career was progressing.

He still does the style of work I knew and have referred to.
But he and a friend produce prints for sale to hotels and motels.
They're quick, easy to make, sold cheaply **AND** he finds them fun.
The artist and his friend; often collaborate on the same work.
They use a nom-de-plume, so no worry about who created a work.
This also means no repercussions where his normal work is sold.

This artist makes more money from these than anything he does.
That includes at galleries and he finds this a little embarrassing.
Interestingly, he has found the experience helps his 'serious" work too!

Could you think outside the square to introduce a production line?
Say prints, drawings, paintings, whatever, as well as your special works.

Opportunity comes your way and you must decide to take it or not.
Your immediate inclination is to jump at the opportunity.
BUT if you think things through, you may start to discern pitfalls.
Most exhibitions at this gallery have not been successful.

So why should yours be any different?
Will you be able to afford to frame 50 works the gallery owner wants?
Can you complete this many in time and up to your usual standard!
This line of thinking may lead you to reject the exhibition opportunity.
But this is evaluative thinking rather than creative thinking.

It's not wrong; but there may be other angles for consideration.
Just because someone offers you something (an opportunity).
You can still turn it into something else, a different opportunity.
Can you do what is offered and develop it into something better?
The exhibition opportunity could be a stepping stone to something else.

Perhaps it could lead to an exhibition at a more prominent gallery.
Then the initial exhibition will be approached from that perspective.

Paint and exhibit works the more prominent gallery wants.
Try to make your exhibition one that the favoured gallery people want.
Do all you can to make sure their personnel attend your exhibition.
After all it's an exhibition for them.
They won't worry about inadequate sales or space, it's not their gallery.
You works will be the focus.

Similarly if someone wants to buy one of your best works.
You'll be tempted to take the money.
After all, one person's money is as good as another's, isn't it?
BUT the potential buyer is a person of modest means.
They read, garden or similar activities and do not socialize.

Imagine you have another potential buyer.
They're wealthy, in the social set, entertain frequently, and well known.
Which buyer's money would you rather have and why make this choice?

The second person is by far the better person to buy your work.
Whilst their money is the same (or could even be more).
They're likely to generate further sales, because of the social activity.
The social network is a key to unlocking residual sales in years to come.
Also their friends can cope with price rises that you'd want for your work.

Also they have large houses and buy more, and larger, works.

With the first buyer, to get similar spin-offs **YOU** need social functions.
Could you do this, do you want to and do you have the time?
Yes some people's money is considerably better than others!
You can still sell to the first buyer.
Save your really great works for the buyers who give greatest exposure.
Business sales are worthwhile if a work is in an entrance or waiting area
So start planning strategies to make sales to these selected people.

Operate by appointment then you could sort out potential buyers.
This is not usual in galleries, but there are some that do this.
Accountants, solicitors, hairdressers, and other professionals value time.
So you must make an appointment to use their services.
You could also have a section of your gallery open to the general public.
BUT then only at certain times according to your marketing plans.
In other words have people calling when you want them.

2. With a market oriented gallery the focus is on sales.

EXHIBITIONS represent the best chance for BULK sales for you.
So this would be an important aspect of a market oriented galley.
But how could the gallery be set up to focus on sales?
What changes are likely in the physical environment of the gallery?

There needs to be a welcome area.
Here people can have cups of tea, coffee, a drink and something to eat.
They relax prior to an interview with you or your sales consultants.

A preview area is needed too.
Where works for upcoming exhibitions are available but **NOT** on show?
This could be near the Exhibition Gallery.
It might be the same as the welcome area.

The consulting area is important.
You or can meet with clients and ascertain their needs.
Preview and welcome areas are a consulting area but could be different.
There could be a separate area for framing consultations.

VIP area.
This is a special area, set aside for free use by your VIP clients.

An exhibition gallery.
Open to **general public** from **opening until closing** of an exhibition.
From **hanging until opening**, viewing only available **by appointment**.
Small Mini-View galleries show work by other artists, or for hire.
Access to these is **by appointment** only, or by consultation with you.
A resale gallery is available for public viewing at any convenient time.

Sell from McDonald's instead!
Market oriented gallery action could be at McDonald's restaurants.
Perhaps you might prefer a local coffee shop or wine bar?
It would depend on the prospect and where they feel most comfortable.

These venues could be your consultant area.
You can meet with clients and ascertain their needs at these places.
That they are **NOT** part of a gallery set-up makes them better venues.
They would not expect to see paintings and be told about them.
Asking questions would be more natural in this environment.
The more you can find out from a prospective client.
The better chance you have to supply exactly what they want.

A potential client rings and makes an appointment to see you.
At the appointed time you meet the prospect at the chosen venue.
There are **NO** paintings to be seen.
After introductions you offer your guest refreshments.
You both make yourselves comfortable.
Ask them questions to find out about them and their interests.
They might think this strange and want to know where the artwork is?

Reply along the following lines.
This is how I always do things.
I do things professionally, which means I like to get to know people first.

I want to find out what they like and what they do not.
I want to be sure my work is suitable and I am not wasting their time.
I need to know what you're looking for and why you want it.
Then I know what to show you.
This is a pre-viewing consultation.

Ask questions of the prospect.
"I think I have just the work you are looking for, would you like to see it?"
You arrange to meet again, perhaps at a venue of their choice.
At the next meeting show one or maybe two suitable works.
Gauge the reaction to the works and you need to select another or not.
Show a minimum number of works to find 1 or 2 closest their real needs.
You still have all the rest to show on other occasions.

Don't talk about your work, ask questions.

Let the potential buyer talk.

Plan a series of questions to find the payoff they expect.

If their needs met.

3. Would a stand-by system work?

You've heard of the 'stand-by' system that airlines operate.
You turn up early, before the plane you'd like to catch departs.
A stand-by ticket is cheaper than an ordinary one.
But you only get a seat if there's a vacancy.
Possibly not all have been booked or there is a cancellation.

Might a 'stand-by' system operate for an artist?
Obviously it will be different from that operated by the airlines.
It's a way of ensuring a maximum number of seats are occupied.
Even if some are not attracting full price (but still profitable).

How could a "stand-by" system help with selling from your gallery?
They say, "If you decide to sell that, I'd like first chance to buy it? "
Then say you have a 'stand-by listing' for when you finish each work?

You put those people into a priority order.
First opportunity to buy something that is desired is a powerful add-on.
Link this to your stand-by system and no need to discount price.

When people buy a work ask if they'd like to be on a stand-by list.
You can of course phone people up who have bought and do the same.
When they ask what that is, explain your system, along these lines.

Well I like to give my regular clients a break.
As they've already bought one or more of my works.
It's likely they'll like others.
As a reward for their loyalty I give them first opportunity to buy another.
Most people appreciate this.
That's why I have my stand-by system, it's a list of people.
Who'd like first look at new work with an opportunity to buy.

Don't forget the steak-knives?
The more people you have on stand-by the better!

Some new works are scheduled for an upcoming exhibition.
But people will still be able to buy earlier.

It is possible you'll be able to sell many works before that show.
You could even have a sell-out before the show opens!
Your next stand-by list is from people who missed out on buying.
As well as those who bought.

What do people miss out on by being placed on your stand-by list?
In return for early buying choice, they only select from a limited range.
Just those you have finished compared with the final exhibition choice.
They also have to make an appointment to visit you at your gallery.

4. Making the most of your time!

Time management is critical if you are artist AND gallery owner!
You are trying to do **TWO** full time jobs!
It is never going to be easy unless you make efficient use of your time.
That's a **FIRST** priority.

You want to make your gallery an efficient way to sell your works?
When you are open anybody can come in.
What's wrong with that you might say?
It is an inefficient use of **YOUR** time to wait in case someone comes in.

Do you have time to do all those things you know you must do?
As well you will need the time to do the ones you'd like to do?
Here's a way to analyse your time and how you spend it.

First thing to do is write all the activities you do in a typical month.
Include things you're committed to, intend to do, or just would like to do.
List them one under another on the left side of a sheet of paper.
Include sleep, meals, hobbies, health care, sport, classes, study.
Also reading, relaxation, meetings, AND painting, grocery shopping, etc.
Try to think of everything.

In a column next to the activities write the time it takes to do each.
This is for a typical day but round the times to the closest quarter hour.
In another column note the number of days a month for each activity.
Some will be every day, but others will be as little as only once a month.
Put the total monthly time in another column next to the previous one.
Multiply time of each activity per day by the days a month it is done.

Calculate the total time you need, to do everything on your list.
Add the numbers of the last column.
Compare this number with the average hours available in a month.
A month is 4 weeks, 22 workdays, 8 weekend days a total of 30 days.
That means there are 728 hours available each month.

Different total needed and hours available is credit or deficit time.
If there is a time deficit, then changes **MUST** be made to your use time.
You really have no choice.

But how do you run your gallery AND an art career as well?
You must actively **MAKE THE TIME** to achieve goals in **BOTH** areas.
Otherwise you will never reach them - it's as simple as that!
BUT how do you find the time?
You're already busy with everything else in your life as well as painting?

Finding the time is about how you set your goals.
The main reason people fail is they have no clear direction.
They follow one idea after another with no clear path to success.
Often they never see anything through to completion.
It's also why people fail once a business has started!
You'll **NEVER** achieve any success if you spend time off in all directions.

Set measurable goals with specific timelines for yourself.
Have carefully thought-out action plans to help you hit those goals.
You'll achieve success faster than you would have thought possible.

Set your ultimate 3-5 year goals.
Ask yourself in 3-5 years, what do you want your life to look like?
What do you want your finances to be like?
What do you want your art businesses to be like?
Think big -- but stay within reason!
Rome wasn't built in a day... or in five years, for that matter.

Those goals need to be measurable.
Instead of "I want to be rich!" -- come up with an actual dollar value.
How much money do you want to make from your art in 3-5 years' time?
THAT'S the goal you should be aiming for.

Set annual goals.
Break down where you want to be in 3-5 years to manageable goals.

Take a look at what you want to achieve in the next year.
What do you need to do in 365 days to achieve your 3-5 year goals?
Write down as many goals as possible.
What are the top 5 things you **MUST** do to achieve your ultimate goals?
Answer this question and you have your top five goals for a year.

Set quarterly goals for those yearly goals still seem pretty big.
To achieve them, break them down into more realistic milestones.
Your quarterly goals you should do every three months.
That means set new quarterly goals in January, April, July, and October.
At the start of a quarter see how you managed your last goals.
Decide what to do over the next three months to keep on track.

Set your monthly goals.
Determine the top 5 goals for every month to hit your quarterly goals.

Set your weekly goals.
What things that must happen this week to hit the monthly goals?
Don't limit to five weekly goals - sometimes fewer - sometimes more.

Set your daily goals.
Each morning list things that must happen that day then check emails.
These tasks should be driving you toward your weekly goals.
It doesn't matter if you have only an hour a day to spend on your career.
Set goals and focus on the really important things you need to achieve,
You'll be surprised how much you can accomplish in a very short time.

But you still need to MAKE THE TIME.
Spend two hours a week building your business - better than nothing!

Once you have all your goals down on paper, don't file them away!
Make sure you can see them in a number of different places.
Tack them to the wall of your office or studio.
Put them on your fridge, beside your TV, even beside your toilet!
You need that constant reminder.

The only person accountable for hitting those goals is YOU.

Start setting those goals **NOW**.

Follow this system and in 30 days surprise yourself at progress made!

5. Time management gets things done!

There's not time to do everything you want to do, and must do.
You spend time fighting crocodiles, but the real task is drain the swamp.
Over the years I've gleaned a few ideas about managing time.

The main thing is do important things first, so they don't bank up.
Most people tend to do the urgent things first.

Urgent and important aren't necessarily the same thing.
The difference of important and urgent is the key to time management.
Here's a matrix to illustrate the idea.

URGENT	NOT URGENT
1. Crises	2.Preparation

IMPORTANT

Pressing problems,	Crisis prevention.
Deadlines,	Values clarification,
Major project	Relationship building,
True recreation.	

3. Interruptions,	4.Trivia,

UNIMPORTANT

Some calls, mail,	Some mail, time wasters,
Some reports,	Some phone calls,
Some meetings,	Many pleasant activities.
Many popular activities.	Busywork,

Success in business lies in Box 2. IMPORTANT but NOT URGENT.
There's a tendency to put off these things.
It almost goes without saying; we do the things required in Box 1.
But, we **MUST** pay attention to Box 2 as well.

There's also a tendency to do too much of Box 3.

URGENT but **UNIMPORTANT** can be put off until later, but often isn't.
Usually these things are urgent for other people but not yourself.

Box 4, UNIMPORTANT and NOT URGENT.
Need not be done at all in many cases.

Another classic time management idea is to use 'To Do' Lists.
It sounds a bit odd, but it's quite logical really.
Just make lists of things you have to do.
The lists might be on paper or even in the computer.
There are pocket organizers which could be used for your To Do List.

Prepare your To Do List each day for the next.
Make a habit - do your list before going home each afternoon (or night).
If it's not possible, or you work at home, do it at night for the next day.
Using this process you can sleep on the actions required.
Many problems will solve themselves overnight.

Highlight the priority items.
The matrix above will give you an idea about what to do.
Obviously the **IMPORTANT** and **URGENT** area contain priority items.
Don't forget about **box 2** though.
Put some of these into your To Do List each day.

At the end of the day cross off items which have been completed.
Then make a new list for the next day.
This way your priorities are clearly focused.

Chapter Five: Where do students come from?

1. Is teaching about influencing others?

2. Past relationships can be hidden assets.

3. Can you increase your teaching contacts by networking?

4. Is word of mouth advertising best?

1. Is teaching about influencing others?

Just how do you influence other people?
If you know the answer to this question you can sell anything!
Influence thoughts and actions of others, done wisely is a success key.
This applies to teaching as well as selling.

Now this isn't anything particularly profound, it's quite simple.
Even children know what to do, and do it quite intuitively!
Seen a child gain a favour from a grandparent - pleasant or aggressive?
Basically that's the secret of influencing others, always be agreeable.

But of course you must be sincere.
That's not hard, for everyone has features that are worthy of admiration.
Even better, is to praise, show concern and appreciate.
People you treat agreeably find good qualities, they didn't see before.

Your behaviour doesn't have to be complicated or devious.
A smile and a handshake may enough in many circumstances.
Extending a helping hand when it is needed will be enough too.
Small acts of kindness are appreciated by the receiver and returned.

Who do you want to influence?
Well educating clients is generally considered a good thing - but is it?
But maybe you spend a great deal of time educating potential clients?
You tell about your methods, materials and techniques.
BUT without making the sales to match the effort?

Is there something wrong with your selling methods?
Is there a marketing solution, well of course there is.
There's a marketing solution to every marketing problem.

You may actually be doing everything back to front.
Do not try to educate clients unless you are being paid for teaching.

The more you explain and educate, the less you sell.
What do you do if you meet a prospect and don't want to explain?
Ask questions, that's what - it works.

Answer their questions with questions.
For example, if they ask – How do you teach?
You reply – How do you reckon (or however you might normally speak)?
Whatever they say respond with – that's pretty close to the mark.
Then ask another question.

The less you tell the more you sell.
For an artist, that's not easy and it's harder for a teacher.
The trouble is, you know too much about what they want to know.
You enjoy recounting this to interested listeners - but it's a trap!

Whoever asks the questions controls the communication.
If they ask the questions (and you answer) they'll eventually be satisfied.
That's it, end of story, but no sale.

There are of course some questions that are better than others.
But any question is better than telling.

You'll find out a great deal by asking questions.
What they want to buy, if they can afford it, and will they **BUY NOW**.

You never get this information by talking, but without it NO sale.
So gallery people who don't know much about you and your works.
Are worth their weight in gold, if they ask questions (which the best do).

Teaching is very much the same.
What do you teach?
Teach what you know.
Use your own experience.
Use other people's experience.

No one product or service can appeal to everybody.
It's the same with your courses too.
There are always people who want something that's not what you do.

Attempts to please everyone is the biggest single mistake.
That's also why you need to be careful when you listen to people.
Do they want something different and are steering you in that direction?
If so, be polite but take no notice.

It's better to decide what you do and get on with it.
Don't worry at all about those who want something different.
No politician tries to appeal to everyone.
With little more than 50% of the vote needed at elections, none does.
So why should you try to cover all bases?

In a business sense you compete with specialists at every turn.
Basically trying to have a broad appeal is a road to nowhere.
Decide what you really want to do and focus on that.
It's best to be something than a jack of all trades but master of none.
Focus according to your interests and skill and you'll improve constantly.
This is the way to keep the learning curve ever moving upwards.

Positioning is capturing a place in people's minds.
Who exactly are you and what do you stand for?
Established companies have a hard time changing market position.
Assess competition and reposition yourself in a way that sets you apart!

2. Past relationships can be hidden assets.

Make an inventory of your past relationships.
Go to past students, old friends, acquaintances, and galleries supplied.
Are there any other past relationships you can think of?
Carefully scan your past for relationships, for new opportunities.
Open new contact possibilities, make an offer to someone you know,
They become students or know someone else who might be interested.

This process is one of gaining referrals.
Enthusiastic students who refer people to your class are best friends.
Thus a well-thought out marketing plan, creates a growing following.

A potent sales tools is unbiased third party testimonials.
To sell classes from your website you must have testimonials.
They give you credibility - no sales literature generates – it's that simple.

So do you collect testimonials?
Get into the habit -a bit like collecting autographs!
Once you have good testimonials, include them where best suited.

Contact students to ask them how they're enjoying the class.
It is easy for a satisfied student to record an audio or video testimonial.
Many volunteer, but ask and you'll get better quality testimonials sooner.
Just collect them and worry about how you'll use them down the track.

Are you trying to sell your course without much success?
If you're not using testimonials, then add them to your present method.
Discover the difference between testimonials and none!
You **will** sell **MORE**.

Testimonials establish your credibility and win potential students.
They're impressed by what people like themselves say than anything.
Yes even than winning a major award!
So never underestimate the power of a good testimonial!

Good testimonials describe how your teaching helped someone.
For example how they became more successful as an artist.
Use testimonials that build your credibility as a teacher.

They should answer questions like:
Was the content of your class accurately represented on your website?
Were you responsive to student needs?
How did their student experience compare with your competitors?
Students want to know if you keep your promises and deliver results.
Testimonials that clearly show those results, as specifically as possible.

More testimonials = more sales!
There are ways to use testimonials effectively and ways that don't!
Prospective students don't want to hear how nice you are.
I'm sure you know lots of nice people you'd never buy from.
That's, because their products don't offer any real value to you.

But use testimonials that offer real MEASURABLE results.
Avoid "feel good" testimonials from students gushing how great you are.
Saying how much they love you but no mention results from your class!
Choose testimonials that tell exactly what they can expect to gain.

Keep your testimonials SHORT and POWERFUL.
Testimonials over 4-5 lines, most prospects skim or skip over them.

Keep them short and get to what matters.
Then you'll also get to what matters for you, results!

Use the most EFFECTIVE formats.
There are different formats you can use to present your testimonials.
This list is arranged from most effective to least effective:
Video testimonials
Audio testimonial with photo of student.
Written testimonial with photo of student.
Written testimonial

Use your website to attract students.
Reviews and comments from satisfied students increases credibility.
It also encourages sales from first-time student prospects.
It can convince readers your teaching **DOES** exactly what you say.
This is particularly important if you are fairly new to art teaching.
So you don't yet have a widespread teaching reputation.

Put your best testimonials on your homepage.
Insert some testimonials in the middle of your sales copy.
A page on your site that features only testimonials is less effective.
People can skip this page or many of the testimonials).

Testimonials on each website page are more effective.
Then they can be relevant to that page - it's that simple!

To encourage new testimonials:
Add a link to a website form for students to give a vote of confidence.
For example, "Click here to tell us what you think!"

Testimonials have a first initial and last name of a satisfied student.
BUT that's **not** enough to fully establish a testimonial giver's credibility.
Every testimonial should have a first name, last name, and location.
They prove recommendations are coming from real people.

Include as much information as possible:
First name
Last name
City, State/Province
URL if they have a web site
Also other relevant information students let you publish on your site.

But you MUST have permission to use testimonials.
Also you need to consider a student's privacy (particularly the internet).
Against providing sufficient information for your prospect's needs.

So when students send you glowing praise in a letter or email:
Contact them to ask permission to add it to your website or promotion.
Do this, even if at the time you don't know exactly where you'll use it.
But there's always somewhere that's appropriate.

Virtually every buying decision is based on trust.
Trust is generated through personal relationships.
Build an ever-growing base of positive referrals.
You'll leave rivals in the dust.

If you don't have any testimonials yet:
Offer a service free to a group of students.
In exchange for their thoughts.

3. Can you increase your teaching contacts by networking?

Before you start any teaching.
Is there a clear understanding of exactly what, how and whom it's for?
Why do prospective students choose your courses over other teachers?

To get a clear understanding of these issues write them down.
Ask someone to read what you've written to see if they also understand.
They may or may not agree with it of course, but that's different.
If you don't understand what you do, how do you expect anyone else to!

Consistent word of mouth referrals depends on relationships.
Identify people already known who can be a foundation of your network.
They needn't attend, but must be willing and able to talk about them.
You will need to help them do this though.

In any social group there are always the talkers.
You are seeking people who talk freely with your target clients.
They do not need to actually attend your classes.
You'll need to do quite a bit of thinking and some talking yourself.
When you come up with some good talkers, it will be worth the effort.
In some cultural groups the main talkers are priests!

Learn more about your networking prospects.
Then you can enhance the relationship by serving their needs.
Find out about the talkers, and what they need.
Their needs may be as basic as being the first one to know something.
Then they can't help talking about it to anyone they think is interested.

You can enhance this, by being a supplier of information to them.
There'll be information about yourself and your forthcoming classes.
But tell them about other things you may discover, from time to time.
The more people you have out there talking, the better.

Help motivate your networking prospects.
There are many ways you can help motivate your networking prospects.
The main way is establish a relationship that develops classes for you.
You help them and they'll help you.
Make them important and privy to inside knowledge, is all that's needed.

Activate your networking prospects.
Develop a system to not just build your referral network, but activate it.
What are the triggers to get people talking about you and your classes?

You could put on a function just for the networkers.
Include drinks and nibbles, it's a special occasion, so don't sell anything.

Over the next few days they'll sell for you.
Networkers who introduce students get special confidential incentives.

Evaluate the results.
How effective is your networking?
How do you know?
There are many types of referrals, some give better results, than others.
If you track your referrals you'll know which works best for you.
Questions of your networking team should give excellent feedback.
Work out how you can improve and then do it.

Are you a contact hub?
You are the hub of a wheel and spokes radiate out to the rim.
The spokes are your referral network.
The rim is those whom you don't know but are about to know about you.
Develop this concept as a basis for your art teaching business.

Can you speak on yourself and classes for about ten minutes?
If prepared you're ready if someone asks and you weren't expecting it.
But if you can't do this, how can you expect your network to do it either?
Then they'll talk, but not necessarily what you'd like to hear.
Prepare yourself and you can prepare your network.

If you attend social or business functions, how well do you mix?
These are prime opportunities to develop networking contacts.
Often there's not time to convey a clear message on what you do.
Just saying "I'm an art teacher," is not sufficient.
Have a one-minute message on what you do and why it should interest.
Try a short message out on a few people before you get it right.

First impressions can be lasting impressions.
We really only have one chance to make a first impression.
Is your first impression one you're happy to give a prospective student?
This may mean you are relaxed and quite natural.

It doesn't mean pretend you're different from who you really are.
If you're shy, there's nothing wrong with that, if you tell people.
Then they'll help you.

Have you thought about your business image?
Many don't, they've an artist image not necessarily good for teaching.
Use marketing knowledge for an identity appealing to intended students.
Teach painting domestic animals and you're in a local cat or dog club.
Provide the media with newsworthy articles on a regular basis.
Show links for what you teach and the most suitable business image.

You must ask too.
People often forget to provide referrals.
This doesn't mean they are unwilling.
Ask people for referrals and show your appreciation.
Even create incentives to go with this.

People want to help you.
Ask if they know someone interested in your class.
A good time to do this is at the time of an enrollment.
If you forgot, then phone the student a few weeks later.
Ask how the new class is.
Then find out if any of their friends would be interested in the classes.

How many ways do you use to generate 'word of mouth' publicity?
Then develop a series of strategies to improve on this start.

4. Is word of mouth advertising best?

Everyone knows this is the best kind of advertising.
It's also the least costly.
Except if it is negative and then 'word of mouth' can be very expensive.
If 'word of mouth' is measured for its effect, it works harder and better.
Than advertising, publicity, sponsorship or any other way of promotion.

Does this mean there's nothing you can do is it like fate?
Do you do the best you can hoping they say something good?
There are many artists who actually think this.
So they consider exposure is all that's needed to start people talking.
Well, there are plenty of things you can do.
Let's start with those people you already know, your present students.

The best ideas are often very simple.
Target talkers - people who talk easily, fluently and frequently.
Hairdressers, taxi drivers, and those with people contacts are talkers.
They are just the people to spread the word about your new classes.

A nightclub, opened full and stayed full with little marketing.
They put on a party for hairdressers just a few nights before opening.
There were queues on opening night.
As most students tend to be female that's an avenue to follow.
Couldn't you do something almost the same?
They talk about your classes as their customers will be your students.

You want people who often meet clients like your students.
Theatre people could fall into this category.
They are usually talkers and often their patrons are also art buyers.

Target networks of influential talkers and reach hard to get people.
Service clubs Rotary, Apex, Lions, BPW, View are people networks.
They meet on a very regular basis.

Many non-English speakers rely on community leaders.
Often they are asked for advice quite outside their areas of expertise.
Doctors, solicitors, teachers and priests are often leasers.
List people like this in your area, then supply them with information.

Find out the talk networks of your present students.
Ask them which organizations they belong to, for example.
Find clubs, industry groups, sporting bodies, religion, political affiliation.
What talk shows do they listen to or look at?

People who aren't your students are likely to be in similar groups.
Link up with them and offer to talk to these groups.
Many are always looking for guest speakers.

Do you remember your student's names?
This can lead to word of mouth' publicity, as they tell friends about you.

Ask them to tell you of anyone who wants to know of classes?
You should!
Most teachers tend to assume that people will talk to others naturally.
But there are many people who don't think of telling anyone about you.
Even more importantly to you about them.
How about, for one week, ask everybody in your classes this question?

Tell me anyone who'd appreciate knowing about my art classes?
Perhaps your family, circle of friends, neighbors or business associates.

Don't be shy; just ask in a polite, but direct manner.
Write down all names, addresses, email addresses and phone numbers.
At the end of the week have a look at what you have collected?

Ask yourself whether it was hard or easy?
Did anyone object?
If you get the sort of responses that I expect, you'll just keep on doing it.
Asking for referrals will become second nature.

You can ask every time and to begin with that's a very good idea.
People you see regularly need to be treated a little differently.
So here's what to do then.

If there's a change in a relationship, then ask for referrals.
Once again, ask for actual names and addresses (remember email).

The change may be someone indicates they're not interested.
Ask for referrals of people they know who might be interested.

You should ask because you're not likely to see them again.
They'll provide referrals as they're guilty about not wanting your classes.
It's a win/win situation.
They're less guilty and your names and addresses are of real prospects.

When someone enrolls, that's also a good time to ask for referrals.
They'll be happy with themselves and glad to provide extra people.
Again you both win.
It may be possible for the referrer contact new people on your behalf.

In an ongoing situation and you're trying to gain an enrollment.
You don't really want to tempt fate by switching to referral seeking.
It might just lose you the one in front of you.

Decide what you are going to say when you ask for referrals.
Put your script into practice for a week and see what happens.
How many different ways do you now use to generate 'word of mouth'?
So you can measure the result to see which is working the best!

Chapter Six: How do you keep students?
1. I receive emails from artists from all over the world.

2. Follow up new students immediately and own them for life.

3. Is there a system for developing student loyalty?

4. Should you have a database then?

1. I receive emails from artists from all over the world.

In many of them the artist writes about their passion for their art.
There is nothing they want more than get in front of an easel and paint.
Maybe you share this emotional attachment with your art too?

But as a teacher there is a business to run.
This takes time from the studio but it has to be done.
Maintaining the passion is now harder rather than easier.
The passion can easily flicker at this point.

An artist doesn't mean you understand how to be in business.
Being an artist is not necessary for running a successful art business.
If this were not so then how could galleries and agents survive?
You don't even need to be an artist to be an art teacher.

But you do have to know how to make the business work.
Any art business must operate according to what it needs to flourish.
The function of any business is to find and keep clients.
The function of a teaching business is to find and keep students.

If you bring students back you don't need to always find more!
It is easier and cheaper to have repeat students than find new ones.
You know who they are, how to contact them and what they know.

All you need to bring them back for more is a small free, service.
Naturally it's best if that something costs you very little.
Here's an example to illustrate the idea.

A gallery gave clients complimentary, 'home made' chocolate cake.
They didn't know the 'throw away' gift created total devotion and loyalty.
People went miles out of their way to visit the gallery over other.
Just because of the free chocolate cake!
Without trying they created a powerful device to forge client loyalty.

So loyalty programs don't have to mean 'fly-buys'!
An apartment complex owner gave tennants free weekly car detailing.
They were at 100% occupancy – the competition averaged only 77%.
With similar pricing, locations, access to schools and transport.
Just for the cost of a few kids, who lived in the complex, to wash cars.
The property earned tens of thousands of $ extra rent competitors lost!
What a great idea!
I've heard of motels doing the same.

We had a rocking horse in our gallery.
Children brought parents to the gallery, just to have a ride.

How can you do this for your art class marketing?
It shouldn't be hard just think of something you can give to people free.
It could be cake, lollies, biscuits or something like that.

You could even offer a number of services!
Give something they like so they study with you rather than competitors.
Cakes and rocking horses had nothing to do with an art gallery.
You just have to find something people will like and you can afford.

But remember, what you give away doesn't have to be art related.
Think of your student market and come up with something they'd like.
Brainstorm ideas for providing something free for them.
So you can now try the best of these for an extended test period.

2. Follow up new students immediately and own them for life.

That's how important follow up is!
It's the most important thing you can do for a strong student base.
Here's a letter you could write:

Dear

*You attended my art class to-day for the first time. Because people who
are my students are important to me, I am writing to you personally and
thanking you for this first time.*

*To commemorate that I want to invite you to return again for the next
lesson/workshop/whatever, and here's what I suggest:*
Here you'll offer a bribe.
*Remember there is less need to make money now to a potential regular
student.)*

*And, I'm not going to impose a time limit. I simply want you to
experience the eventual joy of creating your own quality artworks. I
know through past experience that if you'll come back again, there's a
90% probability you'll return regularly. I am prepared to forego entirely
the profit I'd normally make on your first lesson, to help this happen.*

Yours etc.

Vary this to suit your own focus, but the idea should be obvious.
After three sales they're students for life not just people who come back.
That's worth some effort!

It's great when someone is referred to you by a previous buyer.
The person referred has been 'sold' on your class and your job is done.
But the worst part is waiting for this to happen.
Well you don't have to wait; you can do things to make it happen.

How could you make every one of your students a satisfied one?
So enthusiastic they'll return again and again to your classes.
AND they'll send new students your way too?
Sounds like a system for continual courses doesn't it?

Student service, anywhere means the student is number ONE.
Your classes are absolutely no different.

There are proven ways to do this, which include:
Reducing the risk for your students.
Going the extra mile.
Providing exceptional after-sales service.
Personalizing your offers.
Listening to your students.

Students come back if you provide more service than expected
It's sensible to go an extra mile with something adding value to learning.
Sometimes a little cost, but a payoff is extra referrals and repeats.
But there are times when an extra service costs nothing – like a smile.

List all the extra services you provide your students (or could).
Make sure your students know about them too.
A service they don't know about is no service at all.

Just to start you thinking here are some possibilities:
Arrange framing of their finished work.
Provide a sturdy carry-bag, with your logo, to take the workshop stuff in.

Like most people your students are probably busy.
Although it may not seem so when they come to your class.
If you can do anything to make their lives easier it will be appreciated.
That is worth paying more for.

So as well as classes, provide extra convenience for your student.
Turn a routine into a pleasant and painless experience for students.
This could be as simple as providing an after lesson cup of coffee.

You could advertise some of your extra services, but not others.
New students are surprised with an extra bonus they didn't know about.
It's definitely worth doing.

Just calculate the cost.
For a few extra $ one new student becomes a delighted new student.
That same student is worth hundreds or thousands in lifetime value,
The mathematics make sense don't they?

Provide excellent after sales support and you'll over-deliver.
Teachers' mistake thinking their job is done after the first enrollment.
Artists and galleries make this mistake too.
But nothing could be further from the truth.
A quick after first lesson email or phone call to check if all was OK.
Such a gesture can really be appreciated by students, old and new.

You can relieve feelings of "buyer remorse" they might have too.
Reinforce positive feelings about you and your art classes.
Check with your students and find out a lot about how they think.
So you refine what you do (maybe) and your marketing (probably).
You can also head off any problems before they become complains.

How do you build a more personal relationship with your students?
Listen to their concerns and act on them.
Do not ignore students when they complain or raise a concern.
To not do anything to remedy this is a sure way to destroy a reputation.

Students are reasonable, know things go wrong or mistakes made.
Sometimes things happen that were simply unavoidable.

But they still like you to acknowledge that you've made a mistake.
They like to know you'll do your best to prevent it from happening again.

That's why good restaurants will give you a free bottle of wine.
If your meal is late, or provide a free dessert if your order wrong.
They'll replace a poorly prepared dish, with no questions asked too.
If they didn't do these things, would you go back?
You'd probably tell your friends too.
So the lost business is worth more than a bottle of wine.

If one of your students complains what should you do?
Don't hide but make it easy for someone to contact you with a concern.
Remember the student is always right, so don't argue just listen.
Be quick to acknowledge and apologize for any mistakes.
Tell them what you do to remedy it.
Make sure it won't happen again.
Not empty apologies so use judgment about a refund or compensation.

Sometimes acknowledging a mistake and apologizing is enough.
But the cost of **NOT** listening to your students can be severe.

If your student service is really good you might even charge more!
Your students will pay the extra for those services you provide.
At the very least you could test this idea.

Keep students happy makes your job easier and more profitable.

3. Is there a system for developing student loyalty?

Your teaching career can be built on loyal students.
It's important to remember them so a system is a great memory aid.
Then you just never forget these very important people.

Know your student and find more like them.
Turn students into your biggest advocates, they find others like them.

Do you have loyal students?
What can you do to make sure they stay that way?
Add value by helping your students to remember you in a positive way.
Become a service partner with your students.

You cannot contact someone too much.
Timing is the key to everything.
You don't know if timing is right for a particular student, so just persist.
Sooner or later it will be spot on!

Find ideas to stay in touch regularly, and then do them.
Schedule a working frequency of contacts for your students.
Test the waters before plunging in.
Is what you want the same as what your student wants?

Many teachers maintain contact by a regular newsletter.
A single page or more elaborate, but the regular contact matters.
The majority of the newsletter should be items of interest to the reader.
Only a small amount relating to things that are important to you.
Is your newsletter like this?

Seminars for students:
Conduct a seminar on anything your students would be interested in.
To find out what is of interest, just ask.
Have other people as speakers (trade, suppliers, authorities, etc.).
The focus must interest the audience otherwise they won't come!

Informed students prove the 'find/flog/forget' tactic doesn't work.
It's expensive as you continually find new students and that takes time.

4. Should you have a database then?

Collect the names and addresses of each of your students.
Also names and addresses of anyone interested in your workshops.
Now you can contact any student or prospective student.

You should thank them to show you appreciate their support.
Let them know from time to time about special exclusive opportunities.
These won't be available to the general public.
Give something for their friends who might be interested in their class.
The something is returned to you so you can contact the new person.

So you should have a database.
The main purpose of having a database (or mailing list) is to use it.
Here are a few things you can do:

To get new students for your classes or workshops.
Your present database won't do this if it only contains past art buyers.
Your art students are likely to be different people.
They want to learn to do what you do rather than buy it.
By building your student list, you reach out to new people.

To keep the students you have.
Keep contacting so they don't go elsewhere if they forget you.
Regular contact is necessary.

Fire your students up so they attend more classes.
You can also cross-sell or up-sell by suitably targeted contacts.
Cross-sell is to sell related products to their original purchase.
Perhaps you have art supplies available?
Up-sell' is more expensive or larger quantity than an original purchase.
Maybe you could organize a painting trip to the Greek islands?

Lapsed students can be reactivated.
Don't write anyone off, they may be saving money or ready to spend.
You can nudge them in your direction by maintaining contact.

Your teaching future is cultivating and communicating effectively.
You build a relationship and encourage people to be involved more.
This implies an ongoing, not one off approach.
So you need to build a business so both you and your students benefit.
You can be pro-active about your future.
It doesn't have to be left to chance or fate.

When should you follow up your students for maximum returns?
When is the best time to offer backend products, more lessons?
It's when you're given a natural opportunity to follow up with them.
Here are some examples of what I mean:

You can follow up after enrollment:
Right after someone buys lessons send them a "thank-you" message.
The message includes an offer for a related product.
For example, you could offer your students an art materials package.
This could be through a company that provides you with a spotter's fee.
This is a special package deal on art supplies they need for the course.
But it could also be a special deal on a painting trip to the Greek islands.

An enrollment anniversary is an easy way to follow-up.
Send an offer one month, six months, or a year after they first enrolled.
With classes a year might be too late but 9 months just right.
It all depends on the duration of your program.

Email them to ask how they're enjoying the painting lessons.
Let them know you've got more follow-on classes at a special prices.
The early-bird fees are only being offered to present students.

Follow up whenever you can provide new products or information:
Say sell art supplies, and you've received new watercolour paper.
Contact watercolour or acrylic paint students and offer a special price.
There's a good chance they'd be interested in a quality paper.

There is an important thing to remember with backend products.
Your offers **HAVE** to be things your target market is interested in.
But if you segment your list properly that should not be difficult to do.

Chapter Seven: Professional teaching means money.
1. Do you really want to make money?

2. Your art knowledge can become regular income?

3. Ask for your money up front.

4. More money … better work?

5. How can you increase your earnings?

6. Market your courses smarter!

7. Do you work the back-end?

8. Sell classes for higher prices and make more money!

9. Is sponsorship for you?

10. Can you guarantee your teaching?

11. Gain income by increasing the size of each transaction!

12. Can links to celebrities be a powerful marketing force?

1. Do you really want to make money?

Most people want to make money, particularly if professionals.
There's nothing inherently wrong with wanting to make money.
You'll only be poor if you give up.
The important thing is to try, and having tried, keep going.

All products and services are solutions to somebody's problem.
That's why they're bought!
Never forget this fact of commercial life.

But can you really make money from teaching?
Can you think of artistic problems people have?
Find profitable solutions, which solves the problem for them?
That's how you make money from your art or art knowledge!

You are not likely to learn how to make money in a classroom.
You'll learn by experience for opportunities come and go.
Making quick decisions is an important skill learned in the real world.
Learn life's lessons and move on.
Meet obstacles, give up or get angry, blame others you never make it.

You may need to make sacrifices though.
You need to do some things you'd rather not - ringing potential clients.
But you'll do them because they're on the pathway to your objectives.

If someone else is the problem you have to change him or her.
A very hard task!
It's easier to change yourself and that's what learning is!

Learning is not done by listening or looking; doing does it.
It's much more important to actually do something.
Than talk or read about it or look at someone else doing it.

Most teaching is done by talking.
Write down what you can teach to make money, no matter how small.
When demonstrations are used the learner either listens or looks.
It's like looking at a blank canvas, or paper, before starting a painting.
Anything is possible, including the very best you've ever done.

2. Your art knowledge can become regular income?

The start of each year brings the idea of classes.
You attend, to learn new skills, get new ideas, meet people or refresh.

But you may be thinking of teaching?
It's a way to supplement artistic income and is rewarding in its own right.
The best teachers enjoy it and obtain satisfaction helping their students.

With the qualifications teach in schools, colleges and universities.
If this isn't possible but you still want to teach, or need extra money?
Well that means you'll have to start your own classes.

You can even get the art knowledge from some of my books.
The series that starts with Learn to Copy is a template for a curriculum.
The focus is on learning to paint realistically.

Advantages doing it yourself compared to a formal environment.
You can conduct classes at times to suit yourself so you can still paint.
Teach what you know best, rather than a curriculum from someone else.

But you'll need to remember, it's a business you have, not a hobby.
That means you must receive sufficient money to make it worthwhile.
Only if you are wealthy can you do it as a hobby.

Far too many artists are paid poorly for their teaching.
Usually it's simply because they don't ask enough.
Their price is based on what others charge.
Or because they wouldn't pay more.
BUT why spend hours preparing and teaching.
AND not be adequately rewarded?

Business people pay $hundreds or $thousands, for 1 day courses!
Often these courses are attended by hundreds of people!

Artists don't usually have money to spend like business people.
Business people also better recognise real value in what they learn.

Just to make sure you get the idea, let's do some sums.
A 1-day course attracting 250 people at $250 a head will gross $62,500!
It's possible to advertise the course, provide meals and do a top job.
It's also possible to do it all again next week, somewhere else.
You don't need to run many courses like this to make serious money.

Now compare that with a typical art course.
Artists charge $5 for 3 hour session for 35 weeks earns $175 a student.
Typically this artist starts with ten students as they can't deal with more.
However after 10 weeks there are only five students left.
In this scenario, the artist receives around $1125.
You'd really have to love teaching or be desperate for money?

Somewhere between these extremes there must be a better way.
It may not be possible to obtain business type money.
But you can use some of their thinking, for better money than otherwise.
It's something to think about so what can you do about it?

3. Ask for your money up front.

Most students have to pay for the whole course before they start.
That's what happens at schools, universities, and in business.
If people pay in advance you don't need to collect money each week.
You can focus on your teaching, rather than money collecting.

Paying weekly is a commitment, which is renewed each week.
A subscriber to 'Australian Artist' or the "International Artist' magazine.
That's a longer-term commitment than buying from the newsstand.
The first group must remember to look for a magazine monthly (or 2).

If they forget, they miss an issue.
The chain is broken and more missed issues are likely.

It's the same situation with art classes.
Paying up front for the whole course at the start reduces drop off rate.
This is because students have made a commitment to go the distance.

You have made the same commitment too.
So now you can plan ahead and actually do some serious teaching.

If students pay in advance you receive all the money anticipated.
You can spend a bit to make your course better if you want.
There'll probably still be some drop off to contend with.
There are always external circumstances over which you've no control.
If you're incompetent, people will not keep coming, even if they've paid.
Eventually no-one will enroll in your future courses.
Either way you don't lose money this year.

Paying in advance means people pay more money all at once.
That might be a problem.
It is more difficult to find $500 than $5, particularly early in the year.
Cope with this situation by being more professional.

Provide credit card facilities.

People pay up-front with a credit card at a rate they're comfortable with.

You can offer discounts too.

For example, say you want $600 from each student.

Price your course at $900 and offer 1/3 off if paid before the start.

Many people will find the money to save $300.

Perhaps you could even offer a quite expensive weekly fee?

Then it's not very attractive.

Let's say $35 a session.

If there's 35 sessions in a year, someone paying weekly will pay $1225.

Pay by credit card with an early payment discount makes a great sense.

Point out to them $600 is less than half the price of paying weekly.

Run courses like this and you'll see the few weekly paying students.

4. More money … better work?

Some money is needed to live at an appropriate standard.
If you are not there, like many artists, money is considerably importance.
From a study by the Australian Council for Superannuation Investors.
Chief executive pay has NO link to how well a company performs.

In other words the money paid has no effect on results!
This shouldn't be much of a surprise, it's what most people believe.

If it's not money to motivate people to work effectively what does?
For a possible answer look at the other end of the business spectrum.
A one-man or woman business, and those run by a married couple too.
You know galleries, framing businesses and a many others like this.

These people work very long hours for little money.
Usually less than any employees they may have.
They do all the things a big business does with many less resources.
Yet they keep going against what seems to outsiders, daunting odds.
They don't give up unless absolutely forced to.
Even when in the grip of continuing drought the farmers will still hang in.

People do this because a key element is that there's a dream.
They look for the day when the big wheat cheque rolls in again.
The business is sold for a huge profit and they retire to live in leisure.
Or the business is franchised and on the way to be the next McDonalds.
Or whatever the particular dream is.
People do things others think above and beyond the call of duty.

A small businessperson can make and act on decisions.
That's in spite of the efforts of government these days.
Being your own boss is a major attraction to start and run your business.
It's a very powerful motivating force.

Artists are right in this scenario.
A great time and effort is spent on your activity for it is your choice,
You don't have to do it to please someone else!

Basically people seek satisfaction from what they do.
That's worth more than money.
It's what motivates the best executives and the small businessperson.
If satisfaction is gained greater energy is spent than money as a reward.

But it's also this attitude that keeps many artists poor!
Because satisfaction is great, the profession/career is run like a hobby.
It's for pleasure.

BUT if you believe you've a career.
Then money is a measure of how well you do.
It's not the motivation, that's your desire to follow your dream.
But it does say something about how well you've followed the dream.
It also makes achieving your dream more feasible.

It's unlikely a better income for an artist leads to better work.
They're just like the executives.
But it will lead to a better lifestyle (just like the executives again).
You can live in a garret in poverty or have the lifestyle you'd like.
Either way your work will remain of much the same standard.
The choice is yours.

Your teaching is no different!
So are you paid what you are worth?
You decide the price of your expertise, time and the course itself.
If you don't think that's worth much, fine, then don't charge much.

Fortunately some people prefer paying higher prices for a course.
These people believe they'll be getting a better standard of tuition.
But it's up to you to deliver on their expectation.

It's time for some more sums, to make sure you get the picture.
Your new, well-promoted, course still runs for 35 weeks.
Everyone pays up front, so it doesn't matter if it drops off or not.
You'll receive $6,000 from ten students who receive the 1/3 discount.

You get $6,000 for 10 students, whether it is 3 hours a week or 2.
You'll receive it whether the course runs 35 weeks, or 30, or even 40.
These become items you can adjust to suit your course plans.
If you think two hours is the ideal time, then that's what you do.
If four ten-week terms work out most desirable, then do that.
It's your choice as you charge for a course not an hourly or session rate.

Obviously if you can have more students you earn more money.
Would you like the steak knives too?
Larger classes, or additional classes, can be offered.
Attract people for 8 classes you'll earn $48,000 a year from teaching.
That's a good income for only 16 hours a week for 35 weeks of the year.

OK this could be a fulltime job now.
John Hill (West Sussex, UK) thinks that is the case.
Also considering admin, preparation, set-up and clear-up time.
John also thinks teaching is exhausting.
2 hours in a classroom equals 5 or 6 hours 'normal' work (10 painting).

Unlike painting you get this income all at once at the start of a year.
You can do something with the money to produce even more income!

I'm not saying you should charge the amounts I've suggested.
They are just examples of what is possible.
You could ask for more or less.

Charge more and people assume you're better than everyone else.
Particularly if you charge a great deal more than the competition.
If students think you're better, that's a major factor to actually be better.

The more you charge the better job you'll have to do.
Charge the same as everyone else, they think you are as good as them.

I've tested the ideas suggested here and they do actually work.
Eventually your teaching program determines if people come back.
It will not matter what you charge.

5. How can you increase your earnings?

Everyone wants to increase their earnings, but it's difficult to do.
But if you want to increase your earnings, fees are only a part answer.
You have to sell the workshops or classes too.
A fee structure obviously has an effect on the possibility of those sales.
If all is equal a lower fee has a better chance than a higher one.
But from an income viewpoint, fees have an effect on potential earnings.
If fees are low you'll need to sell many places for a particular income.
BUT the higher fee your class commands; the fewer students needed.

Say you want to earn $20,000 a year (not much these days).
If the average fee for a student is $200 then you will need 100 students!
If your average fee is $1000 then only 20 students are needed.
Which of these options do you have a better chance of achieving?

What other ways can you increase your earnings?
Beyond pricing, there really are only five ways to increase earnings.

Work more hours.
Implicit in this is that the extra hours are productive.
Non-productive are talking, drinking cups of coffee, reading the paper.
So more productive hours worked is an aspect of this approach.
Teach more students, collect more fees but
New courses may not be needed.
There's a limit to the hours available, and also your fatigue level.

Get paid more.
I guess this is self-evident, but it's also easier said, than done.
If you don't ask more for classes, you never get more either.
But you must have a sales base from which to commence this process.
The secret is to provide value for money at all times.
Then even in more difficult times you can ask for more.
Getting paid more can be from higher fees, but also from more classes.

Get others to work for you.
A gallery proprietor can have 20 or 30 artists working, part-time anyway.
Similarly many artists have five or six galleries working, part-time too.
Another way for an artist is to have an agent.
This frees up focus on creative activity, which only you can do.

Sell your intellectual property, as opposed to time.
Some people are paid per hour, others are paid for what they know.
Artists are fortunate, in that they come into the latter category.
Your teaching is a product of your intellect, experience and creativity.
You should earn more than people working an hourly rate (other artists).
But only if teaching or lecturing in your own business (otherwise hourly).

Sell systems.
People who franchise a business sell a system for making money.
Artists don't usually think this way.
BUT you can sell your way of teaching.
Sell your painting methods, write a book about them, and it's a system.

6. Market your courses smarter!

OK how can you sell your classes?

One of the main things you should do is to be really well organized.
You need to market smarter and more effectively in low cash-flow times.

Can you implement a client loyalty program?

Reward people for buying over a certain amount (more than normal).
The reward should cost less than the extra money spent by your client.
You need spending opportunities over and above just the class fee.
This could be supplies, special trips, magazines, or clothing.
Anything suitable for a student.
A visit to your studio costs only time.
Students would spend a little more to see where you create works!
Your imagination is the only limit here.

How good are your cross-selling techniques?

Cross-selling is a buyer also buy another related item or service.
A well-known example is the selling of 'French fries' by McDonalds.
It costs nothing to ask for a sale that wouldn't otherwise take place.
It helps McDonalds profit.
But this is not just selling; it's also providing the customer with a service.
It is appreciated that chips and hamburgers commonly go together.
What can you offer people who attend your classes?
Exhibition, written valuation, framing, whatever you think of at extra cost!

Could you have a feature of the week?

A lesson, valuation, art supplies or something a student hasn't bought.
Have a special offer built around this product or service.
Over time, each different offer attracts a wide range of potential clients.

Can you invent ways to get new students into the classroom?

Host an events day, try new direct mail, be creative with offers.
Run demonstrations or workshops.
One could be a graduation show by present students.

Another might be to visit a class in action.
You need to be 'top of mind' so look at what people do in other areas.
Fashion, sporting goods, life insurance, or other, study what happens.
Develop a version that'll be just right for your prospective students.
John Hill (UK) said door to door flyer distribution good for new clients.

Communicate regularly with students and prospective students.
Don't forget to include former students too!
Keeping in touch is a certain way to get them to spend more.
Keep in touch at least 4 times a year otherwise they start to forget you.
Newsletters do not have to be expensive.
A single sheet written by you in just the way you speak is often enough.
A phone call every few months is even better.

Write to ALL students and prospective students to offer specials?
Writing to all students (present, former, prospective) is worthwhile.
2 for 1 offer, preferred student special, companion products or services.
Also exclusive purchase offers for new products.
These induce sales that wouldn't occur, not re-schedule planned sales.

7. Do you work the back-end?

The back end is where the real money is!
Your initial offer is the front-end.
Any related product you sell people **AFTER** they buy is the back-end.

Once students have bought your tuition any sale is profitable.
Because there is less expense and the student's trust is established.

A back end product is priced 5 to 30 times more than the front-end.
From this it follows that your front end sale could be quite inexpensive.
A back end should be congruent and enhance value of an initial offer.
The back end should make it better, faster, easier or more complete.

The back end helps your students satisfy their needs or wants.
But **NEVER** in such a way to reduce the value of your front end offer.

Many marketers expect ALL the profits to come from the back end.
In fact, most infomercials you see on TV are only front end offers.
A seller breaks even and make **REAL** money on back end products.
That's why your entire marketing campaign includes the back end.

Check Amazon.com for how they make more offers after the first?
These are effective back ends in action.
The last time you went to a movie, did you buy popcorn or a soft drink?
That again is a back end sale.
Now you know about back end offers, you'll see they are everywhere.

The hardest sale you will ever make is the initial sale.
That is precisely why back end products do so well.
The biggest hurdle is earning trust and credibility to make the initial sale.
From that point forward if you have a quality course, it becomes easier.
It's also much more profitable to make subsequent back end sales.

It costs money for a front end sale if you used paid advertising.
It definitely takes much more time to attract buyers with free advertising.
You have limited supplies of both.

The back end is a total win/win situation.
That's because your back end is focused on existing clients only.
Your clients are already in buying mode.
If your back end offer is done correctly, they will be happy to buy it.
They benefit by enhancing their first purchase.
You benefit by making them happier and making more money.
You won't get 100% of clients to take you up on your back end offer.
That's fine for you don't need them to.

What can you do to entice back-end sales?
People don't necessarily know all the things you do, or they could have.

Use signs, posters, demonstrations or workshops.
Here are some backend strategies you can use to expand your profits.

Offer other products or services that complement your initial sale:
As you sell courses, offer your students an art materials service as well.
Offer add-on courses, tours, written reports, speakers, an endless list!
An audio recording of how to hang their completed work.
A student membership program
A newsletter
A "done for you" hanging service
Related products you sell as an affiliate (framing, insurance).

Sell more of the same product or service at a discounted price:
Your students will need more art supplies regularly?
Buy one and get the next one cheaper.
But the best is to sell future courses!

Sell your students an upgrade to their present course:
If they used and liked a basic course, students will consider an upgrade.

Your front-end course is to attract people at a lower price.
A back-end course goes from a beginning to more specialized learning.

You also charge more for the back-end courses.
Educational institutions (universities) use this strategy.

Use paid subscriptions as backend products:
If you're established as an expert in your area, build on your reputation.
A subscription to "premium" information for students, as a backend.
This might be your special news-sheet on how to hang paintings.

Split up your current product:
Your book on oil painting, as an eBook for $9.95 for volume sales.
30 days later, offer students an advanced, expanded printed version.
Home office management and art insurance tips at $29.95 or $39.95.

EBooks are great backend products with high profit margins!
Consider writing a short book on a topic that's related to your course.

You sell a DVD on teaching people how to paint in watercolours.
Sell updated versions to past buyers when the DVD is upgraded.

Offer someone else's product!
A fast **EASY** way to add a back-end is someone's product or service.
You don't have to spend any time or money developing a new product!
Do this in exchange for a percentage of each resulting sale.
If you create new backend products to complement existing teaching.
You need to know how to target the right products to the right students.

You don't have to stop at just one back end offer either!
What if you had **MULTIPLE** back end products?

Successful marketing is all about LEVERAGE.
You need systems but when you want to boost your revenue,
Back end systems give you more leverage than any tactic you can use.

Do you have a back end in place?

How does that change what you can offer on the front end?

8. Sell classes for higher prices and make more money!

They'll be perceived as of a higher quality than the opposition.
Students will boast at attending your courses.
Referrals and word of mouth advertising works for you too.

The psychology of price now works in your favour:
We've always been taught "You get what you pay for".
Price sets up expectations.
PRICE IS a guide to **QUALITY**.

BUT you can deliver more value too:
Ultimately the value you provide dictates profit you receive.

Increase the value and your income goes up.
High-profit courses with high-margins give room for sensational value.
Add high-value extras and deliver truly unique unadvertised bonuses.

You OWN the marketplace if your courses have a premium price:
Then you can afford to pay more to acquire a prospect.

But that prospect is a better prospect.
Say you're competing against someone who only has $10 week course.
You have a $1,000 per year course – there's going to be no contest.
You spend more on advertising, more on testing unusual add-ons, etc.
Your back-end products or services can be high value **AND** high priced!

You can even make bad results work for you.
Let's say you're direct mailing a high-priced course.
Make money with a fraction of the response a low- fee course needs.
The teacher who can spend the most to acquire a student will **WIN**.

Most people undercharge for what they provide.
If your course isn't good enough to raise your price – make it better!
Making it cheaper will not work!

If sales are hard to come by then reducing prices is illogical.
Lower price means you must sell more to make the same return.

But you need people to sell to.
The foundation of an art career is your contact list.
They mainly are from what is termed 'word of mouth' advertising.
People who have enrolled in the past are the most likely to come again.
Their friends and associates are next most likely potential students.
The best source of new prospects is former students.
Can you harness this powerful force?
"Advertising was a waste of money once again, I didn't spend much.
Buyers from my database or VIP's" (Jacqui Hill – Brisbane, Australia)

9. Is sponsorship for you?

It is relevant to have a look at something most artists ignore.
A sponsor is supports an activity pledging assistance in advance.
The assistance may be money, but this is not necessarily the case.
Facilities for classes, work on your behalf, or free ads are sponsorship.

For sponsorship to work there has to be a win-win situation.
A sponsorship arrangement is beneficial for both you and the sponsor.
It's not just about providing money so you do something you want to do.
Share the outcomes so it's not just your workshop but the sponsors.

First thing is select and define exactly why you want sponsorship.
Are you considering publishing a book, lecturing, providing workshops?
Any of these, and many other projects, could be of interest to a sponsor.
However, initially you must decide.
Perhaps it is a workshop on a certain topic?
It could be a class trip to some place of interest.
Perhaps you have a theme that you would like to develop?

Generally sponsorship for a single aspect of your project is best.
Rather than seeking sponsorship for the lot.
May have relationships with a range of sponsors for different activities.
Accommodation, transport, marketing, postage, printing, people,
administrative or materials.

Check the sponsorship fit for your strategic (long-term) vision?
Naturally the sponsorship should align with these.
Get help to do things you want to do.
Rather than do things to get sponsorship.

Who can benefit from this?
Seek sponsors who would benefit from your proposals.
Benefit is more than mention in media and a public acknowledgement.
Those things are just the minimum benefit for a sponsor.

You need to research the needs of each potential sponsor.
Then you might understand what they want from your proposition.

A small amount of background information can be a great help.
For a project, approach all sponsors as potential long-term partners.
Try to find out their strategic plans to know their business direction.
Talk to key people in an organization about where it is headed.
A person who answers the phone knows about people they work for.

Also examine the business climate in the particular industry.
A building industry slump and sponsorship is harder than at other times.
Look for trends in marketing activity too.
This shows competition for a product or service from potential sponsors.

Research to find a way to help a sponsor achieve business goals.
At least move in that direction.
Many people and organizations provide in-kind or financial sponsorship.
Provided they see the strategic benefits in the arrangement.
Sometimes there are sponsors who do not seek any benefit.
But it is still best to approach them with details of what you do for them.

What evidence do you have?
Examples of previous successful results from similar arrangements.
Initially you will not have this material.
Collect it during the first, and subsequent project, sponsored or not.
This might include photos, videos, actual works, maps, newspaper
cuttings, marketing material, statistical data, sketches, plans, and
anything else.
Your potential sponsor gains extra insight into your proposal from this.

Are you business-like?
Tell potential sponsors all arrangements will be confirmed in writing.
It's probably a good idea to do this anyway.
A business-like approach, sponsors like but don't expect from artists.
But you are different, aren't you (well you are an art teacher)?

You successfully land a sponsorship arrangement, so celebrate.
You will have put in quite a deal of effort and deserve of a small reward.

But you'll need to confirm the arrangements with the sponsor.
Prepare a brief written statement of about a page.
Outline what you'll do plus a timeframe for sponsorship arrangements.
Include what the sponsor is to do, and what you provide for the sponsor.
Possibly there will be review dates as well.

Now comes the really hard part.
You need to follow through on your commitments.
No matter what, deliver what you promised to your sponsor, on time.
This includes acknowledging sponsorship arrangement where possible.
Personalized appreciation certificate, in newsletter and press release.
Place their corporate logo on printed material linked to the project too.
A public thank you will help make longer-term arrangements more likely.

Review and evaluate sponsorship near the end of a project.
Decide whether the sponsorship is still aligned with your objectives.
How could it be modified to improve that aspect?
Invite the sponsor to comment on the outcomes from their point of view.
This approach can build a strong partnership with you sponsors.
Regular reviews of all involved is vital for continuing, stable relationship.

10. Can you guarantee your teaching?

Have you ever heard of a course guarantee?
What about offering a guarantee with your course!
Perhaps 'If you don't find this course worthwhile, get your money back.'
Or 'Money back after six weeks if you haven't improved!'
Structure your guarantee whatever way you like, but offer one.

What other art class offers a guarantee?
What other any kind of class or course offers a guarantee?

As soon as you do this your course is above any alternatives.
Most people enroll in a course hoping it will be great.
These high expectations are one of the main causes for dropping out.
Most courses can't meet that unrealistic level of expectation.
Neither can you!

A guarantee helps with this, as it takes people's worry away.
'If it doesn't work out, well I can get my money back.'
They've nothing to lose so a student is relaxed from the start.

This is even better if you link your guarantee to a long time frame.
'Your money back, if after 6 months you haven't learnt something new.'
The pressure is off you and them to start at an unrealistic level.
You can build their skills and knowledge gradually, but surely.

What does your guarantee tell students?
A guarantee also tells people you are confident about what you do.
You wouldn't offer a guarantee unless you were, would you?
A guarantee puts pressure on to perform to student expectation.

What does it do for you?
Even more importantly, a guarantee is a way you'll get more students.
Someone has a choice between two courses, both seemingly equal.

BUT one has a guarantee.
Which one will they choose?
They'll select the course with the guarantee.
Even if more expensive, they get their money back if it doesn't deliver.
It also helps combat non-course alternatives that people might consider.

Offering a guarantee is a very powerful incentive.
This is particularly strong when other people don't!

When can your guarantee apply?
It's up to you as there's a choice between input or output guarantees.

An input guarantee guarantees the input the students will receive.
We'll guarantee you'll receive tuition from a fully qualified tutor, ten
painting trips, no more money to spend (you supply materials), or
anything else.
One possible problem is that other people may provide the same things.
But they don't guarantee to supply them.

An output guarantee is about what they'll receive.
You learn 10 new ways to paint in oils or an outcome considered likely.

How long a period should your guarantee cover?
As long as possible!
Guarantee duration is the time to judge if the benefit was received.

A longer guarantee is more appropriate.
Most benefits from a course take time to appear (need to do lessons)
In addition (say 6 months) there is a good chance people forget about it.
They are now involved in the course anyway.

Keep the first exercise your students do.
Then later that can be compared for course improvement.
Improvement is usually gradual
That's why it often goes unnoticed.

The before/after exercise will highlight what has happened.
This is particularly so if the exercise was the same one each time.

11. Gain income by increasing the size of each transaction!

Simply charge more.
This is one of the easiest ways to get more money.
Instead of new, exciting, and hard ways to get more money.
Here is an old, proven, and easy way to get more money **RIGHT NOW**.
Just charge more.

There is one main reason you should not be afraid to charge more.
People actually believe that if it costs more money it's better.
Wanting the most expensive thing is common behaviour.
Even if they don't buy it because they don't have the money.
They still want it just so they can have it and feel like they're special.
They'll also tell other people!

Think about golf shirts.
There's absolutely no difference between a Polo golf shirt and others.
Except the Polo label and the fact that it is more expensive.
But people still think, "Oh, Polo is better." - **BUT** why?

Because it's more expensive, that's why.
There's scientific research into correlations of wine price and quality.
This research supports the notion that price determines quality.

In art it is no different.
In his day van Gogh's paintings were thought to be inferior.
He couldn't sell any.
What about now?
Have the paintings changed?

Charging more helps increase the size of each transaction.
What if you're afraid to just charge more for the sake of charging more?
You could build more value into your course package.
Add audio components and charge more for an advanced audio edition.
Add an invitation to visit your studio which is worth quite a bit.

Another thing you can do is add more bonuses.
Then lift the price because the perceived value of your offer is better.

Another way to charge more is add scarcity and exclusiveness.
Only allow 5 people to take your painting course and it's very expensive.
BUT those 5 people get more personal interaction with you.
Instant price justification.

Another way to increase transaction value is a deluxe version.
So have a regular version and a deluxe version.
The deluxe version could be a piece of paper with "deluxe" on it.
People would buy it ...just because it exists.
If you provide a standard course then make sure it is low cost and basic.
The deluxe version is much better value (you provide all materials).

12. Can links to celebrities be a powerful marketing force?

The biggest challenge marketers face today is to get noticed?
There's so much clutter people switch off so how do you grab attention?
Celebrities are an **EFFECTIVE** strategy to accomplish this difficult task.
Celebrities provide **INSTANT** attention.

Start by promoting yourself.
For many artists the very idea of self-promotion is anathema.
But if you don't do that, then who will?
A professional must earn a living, involving much more than painting.
Same applies for an art teacher if you want students.
Promoting yourself is an important part of that.

You might not really understand the power of testimonials.
What someone says is 1,000 times more believable than what you say.
SO what a celebrity says about your course or school is powerful too!
It's testimonial on steroids.
Celebrity endorsements give **INSTANT** credibility

Links to a celebrity is a way for higher prices with less resistance.
Would you use just any old exercise machine?
Work-out on the same exercise machine Michael Phelps uses?
People want the exercise machine used by the celebrity.

A high priced product or service is sold by celebrity endorsement.
Price becomes a secondary issue - or even a non-issue.
Celebrity endorsement allows **HIGHER** prices with **LESS** resistance.

How to attract affluent clients least affected by the economy?
You must provide a **BETTER** customer experience than the competition.
There is a chiropractor in San Francisco who used Tony La Russa.
He's the manager of major league baseball's St. Louis Cardinals.
To promote his business.
His patients tell about their chiropractor, a friend of Tony La Russa.

Who would you rather do business with?
Joe Blow or the guy (or girl) who knows a celebrity?

Most will patronize the person who knows a celebrity.
They can tell their friends all about it (which drives more business there).

BUT it does all start with providing a BETTER student experience.

A celebrity has expert status.
Being in the media is instant expert status.
Whether national TV or local newspaper.
They wouldn't be interested in their opinion if you're not an expert, right?

People prefer to do business with a person who's been on TV.
So being featured in newspaper or magazine articles is powerful.
You even have a chance to be that person.
Celebrity is an effective strategy for more **PROFIT** from a course.

Have you considered using a celebrity to boost your courses?
How will you go about it?

Chapter Eight: What do you teach?

1. The lethal combination!
2. There are only two choices if deciding what to teach.
3. Is making mistakes – good or bad?
4. What's wrong with failure?
5. Do you have a graduation certificate?

1. The lethal combination!

You pass something to students for that's what teaching is about!
This might be knowledge, experience, or anything else worthwhile.

You may know Ford Motor Company owned Jaguar (until recently).
Like many car manufacturers Jaguar lost money so Ford rescued them.
This has been a common occurrence in recent years in the car industry.
The following story was in a car industry trade magazine.

Jaguar always had passion.
It was run by people who cared more about Jaguar than their careers.
When Ford brought process to that passion, it was a lethal combination.
'You've got both sides of the brain.' (Mike Dale Chairman Jaguar USA)

Like Jaguar, most artists have passion.
You're probably passionate about teaching too or you wouldn't do it.
That's what drives you and keeps you going!
Without it you'd give up or not even start!
Lack of money, ideas or time are often cited as reasons for failure.
More time, money or marketing ideas without passion is a fruitless effort.

Your passion must be linked to process to attain success.
It's the combination of business skills with your passion that is lethal.
It can make scarce resources work effectively, whatever is available.

So you have passion for your teaching?
Do you have process or systems to put your skills and talent to work?
Just how well do you have things organized?
Do you waste time, money, talent, opportunity or other scarce resource?
Do you have the lethal combination that's crucial to your success?

Let's say you do indeed have the passion.
These ideas could trigger that needed combination of process and skills.
The bigger the changes the bigger the potential gain.
"Imagination is more important than knowledge." – Albert Einstein

This book assumes you have the passion for teaching others.
The focus is on systems to translate your passion to student outcomes.

Do you have the lethal combination?

2. There are only two choices if deciding what to teach.

You either teach what you know.
Or you teach what someone else knows.

Few teachers teach from their own experience.
They access what others have learned.
Books, lectures, film and other media provide this access.
Sometimes there are curricular that set out teaching steps.

A good teacher can teach anything with the right source material.
Good teachers introduce complex understanding to students.
But not all teachers are good teachers.
Not all curricula is equal.
Some is dated and others fiction disguised as fact.

Select part of someone else's stuff and don't teach the lot.
You can do a good job of teaching that to your students.
Other components can become future courses.
Then you'll be able to have the same students returning for tuition.
You'll also offer better courses.

You can even get the art knowledge from some of my books.
The series that starts with Learn to Copy is a template for a curriculum.
The focus is on learning to paint realistically.

The other choice is to teach what you know.
Here your own experience is the basis for your teaching.
Even a relative beginner has had some experience at least of beginning.
They can teach what I learned when I started out or something similar.

With more experience the greater range of courses you can offer.
Think of various things you have done and they can become a course.
How to have a successful exhibition could be one.
Preparing for a field trip could be another.

Courses can even be based on failure.
How not to approach a gallery is an example.
Paint horses better than I did.

If you specialize in something, that can be a focus for teaching.
You paint in oils.
Painting houses.
You sell commissions but do not exhibit.
You are also a picture framer.

What keeps your potential students awake at night?
Can you provide a solution?
That could be the basis for a popular course.

Your courses will then have an authenticity that many others lack.
That's because your own experience is the basis for what you teach.
Start right and keep classes small and expand as you gain experience.

Eventually you are an authority on your particular teaching focus.

3. Is making mistakes – good or bad?

There are many of us who hate making mistakes.
There are also people who regard mistakes as opportunities to learn.
They don't want to make mistakes, but are not afraid if that happens.
They're wiser, more determined often better due to experience.

By making mistakes we learn.
We learn the consequences of what we do.
If you avoid making mistakes, that's probably the biggest mistake of all!
Do nothing and learn nothing.

Yes you learn by making mistakes.
Don't fear a mistake, or seeming foolish, or doing something wrong.
Just do what seems to make sense and see what happens.
I'm probably writing that way right now!
If necessary I'll modify what I have done and see what happens next.
Eventually I'll have something much better than whatever I started with.

It's a process of continual improvement.
I learnt this through my art experiences.
Which have been reinforced in other aspects of my life too.

Many people think they can learn from other people's mistakes.
But the lessons are never the same.
Our own mistakes are special to us and are part of our lifelong learning.
We can never have another's experience.
There's a tendency to repeat the same mistake, if the lesson isn't learnt.
Many people's love life is a testimony to the truth of this assertion.

Learn from a mistake and you're unlikely to repeat it.
That's because you're changed.
You've gained wisdom.
You cannot return to your pre-mistake self.

When you try to learn from others you are not usually changed.
It is easy to return to your past behaviour.

If a mistake has been made people adopt different postures.
Some deny making a mistake.
It was really someone else and blame them.
But they may perceive that there's not really been a mistake made at all.
They justify the mistake saying that it'd never have worked anyway.
But all of these are just avoidance tactics.
They are all barriers to learning from the mistake.

What are your attitudes to making mistakes?
What are the people around you attitude to making mistakes?
Are there some financial or artistic issues that are not resolved?
If you are upset, then what lesson can you learn from that?

What is your attitude towards making mistakes in your teaching?
So you can try alternatives to see if there is any effect on your students.
Do you encourage them to make mistakes so they can learn?

What did you learn from your mistakes?
This can be the basis for your teaching.
Then you can teach from your own experience.

You can also access what others have learned.
Refer to books, lectures, film and other media.
Try out some of what you find and see what happens.

Now you can select a component of someone else's stuff.
Don't teach the lot - just part of what someone suggested and you tried.
Then you can do an even better job of teaching that to your students.

You can teach the other person's stuff as they intended it.
You can also teach what you found out using their ideas.
Keep this distinction clear so your students understand which is which.

Other components can become future courses.

Then not only will you able to have the same students returning.

You have better courses **AND** are gradually based on what you know.

4. What's wrong with failure?

Before deciding what's wrong with failure, what is failure?
If there's a right way to do something, then other ways are wrong.
The wrong way is usually seen as a path to failure.

But often there isn't a right or wrong way, just a variety of ways.
Each having the desired outcome but various other features as well.
Then it's not possible to be wrong, so it's impossible to fail either.
Unless avoiding a choice is a failure but even that is one of the choices!

Say we must do something that has a correct way, but we don't!
That's how we learn what **not** to do isn't it?
It's the beginning of knowing why a different way might work better too.
Do we consider such learning as failure?

In business, bankruptcy is a badge of honour for entrepreneurs.
This isn't to say all business people should go bankrupt!
But many learnt from the experience.
They are better business people as a result.
Of course there are some who didn't learn anything too.

I'm suggesting you only fail if you don't learn something.
It doesn't matter whether you achieve what you set out to do or not.

Avoidance, created by a fear of failure is a behavioural style.
Human Synergistics International in Border Mail 16/08/02 p3.
The reported research took 5 years.
It involved 35,000 principals, managers and CEO's.
It applied to Australian and New Zealand business owners or managers.
They think and behave defensively and create a negative work culture.

A second major trait was conventional thinking.
In other words seeking security within the rules.
The characteristics go together.

Following rules is the way to avoid failure.
Many artists are like this and maybe your art teaching business is too?

Aggressive-defensive behaviour characterized most managers.
They found fault, controlled and competed against others.
If they couldn't avoid it.
Their first thought is maintain security and safety for themselves.
They use self-protective behaviour.
The culture is covering up, avoiding blame, being tough and aggressive.
Apportioning blame is a major characteristic.

Constructive managers were achievement oriented.
They preferred to set their own goals.
They had high personal integrity and encouraged and mentored staff.

But what causes this type of behaviour?
People fear failure and seek security by staying inside perceived rules?
Laws of what can and can't be done in business increase exponentially.
Tax laws are many and so complex no single person is an expert on all!
Add OH&S, industrial relations, financial management and reporting.

An army is supporting the proper observance of these statutes.
A lack of confidence, family pressure, little time, and constant change.
Place their own pressure on a business person, even artist or a teacher.
It's really a wonder anyone takes any kind of business on.

This is the environment your classes operate in.
Possibly it's our modern culture and there's seemingly no end.

I've suggested you only fail if you don't learn something.
People like this won't exhibit those undesirable management traits.
If something leads to unexpected outcome, they learn.
But it's not a mistake.
One should have faith in oneself, but also remember you're not infallible.
Quite the contrary, for that's how you learn.

5. Do you have a graduation certificate?

A graduation certificate marks a conclusion.
This doesn't necessarily mean the student has finished.
It might just mean they have finished one part of something longer.
It also might mean now is the time for a different course.

Also you can have a graduation ceremony.
That is a way to generate local promotion for your courses or school.

Sample Graduation Certificate
If you want something more elaborate, then that's what you should do.
This is a starting point.
Think about the things you'd include on your certificate.
Which means you can now start designing your own.

(Name) has graduated from (title of course and level).

Signed by (teacher):....................
Signed by (head of school):.....................
Dated:.................

Chapter Nine: Teaching methods.

1. All teaching should be structured.

2. One can do art so is it an action?

3. What about the medium in relation to art?

4. The journey is the goal!

1. All teaching should be structured.

Teaching implies that learning is not left to chance.

Unless there is some structure by the teacher there is NO teaching.

The kind of structure will vary according to the desired learning.

But unless the teacher does something then learning is left to chance.

A common form of structure is associated with skill development.

This has been referred to in the previous module.

With learning there is a movement from the lowest level to higher levels.

Teachers do things to facilitate this student learning.

This sequence is very common in sports coaching.

Flexible	Responsive
Effective	Efficient
Control	Predictable
Uncontrolled	Unpredictable

The first factor is the degree of control in ascending order.

At its lowest level skill is uncontrolled and thus unpredictable.

Then as some control is asserted predictability results.

The second factor is results that follow, again in ascending order.

It is also the desired result from teaching or coaching.

The two requirements to move up the ladder are time and practice.
Performance of a task is related to practice at that task.
With practice comes control and we can predict what might happen.
Our past experience lets us do this.
Teaching (coaching) involves structuring these elements.

As we practice we become more effective, and the results improve.
Because we avoid things that lead to mistakes and unwanted outcomes.
Our practice has made us efficient.

Most really good artists work at this level due to experience.
It seems easy to an observer.
At the highest level there's flexibility of performance.
The artist can respond to any situation because of their experience.
Someone can paint portraits, not merely pictures of people, for example.

But developing skill takes a lot of time.
This is obvious observing children learn to play a sport, or read, or paint.
Adults learning the same things are inclined to be impatient.
They tend not to allow sufficient time for skill to develop.
A structure is necessary to provide the needed time.

The sport of body building illustrates what should take place.
The athlete completes many lifts of weights over a long period of time.
Small increments of additional weight are applied at regular intervals.
Eventually the weight-lifter builds sufficient strength to lift heavy weights.
Weights that were impossible at the beginning of the training process.

Skills are basically practiced behaviours.
That's what the experienced weight-lifter has attained.
Artistic skills develop in the same way.

To teach skill development there must be an appropriate structure.
Otherwise there will be inappropriate learning.

Many repetitions allied to small increases in difficulty work best.
For artistic skill 200 small exercises beats 1 or 3 major works every time.

Do you intend to develop skills in your students?
Many repetitions with small increments of difficulty are then necessary.
Maintaining enthusiasm over a lengthy period of time is also necessary.
What will you do about that?

2. One can do art so is it an action?

Teachers have different viewpoints about this.
Their teaching should be and mostly is based on their particular view.
A student should know the teacher perspective before commencing.

The idea that art is an action views art as a process.
Statements like "It is an art" imply a skill or refinement in a process.
Certainly it seems as if some manipulation is necessary for a work of art.
Is art the employment of this skill?

But in an action the medium must be changed in some way.
Usually the artist makes the changes.
But it could be someone else.

Thus manipulation is a necessary condition for the idea of art.
How much manipulation is necessary?

At least sufficient manipulation to realize the artist's concepts.
The person who conceives the operation, is the artist.
Even if carried out and brought into a related form by another.
An example is a sculptor's bronze poured in a foundry by metal workers.

An artist employs others for certain skilled tasks to make a work.
Time-consuming tasks are more efficiently carried out by others.
Architects employs builders, carpenters etc. to construct his office block.
Sometimes the skilled operations may be too complex for the artist.
Technicians and engineers at Sydney Opera House for Utzon's idea.
If skill is a low level it can be entrusted to others (Rubens apprentices).

A craftsman manipulates a medium according to an artist's ideas.
Artist and craftsman may be the same.
But it's not a necessary condition for art.

The artist's knowledge includes the craftsman's skill.
Even though the artist may not possess this specific ability himself.
If the artist carries out both roles, the craft process has a service role.

Employment of manipulative skill by someone is necessary for art.
This may be by the artist or someone else.
Using manipulative skill by the artist is **NOT** necessary for a work of art.

3. What about the medium in relation to art?

The medium is how creativity is expressed in a perceptual form.
The nature of the artist's activity indicates if the process is called art.
The medium is important for deciding what kind of art it will be.
Many mediums can symbolize creativity (words, sounds, movements)
In **ART** the medium **MUST** be visual.

The medium itself may be perceived as the problem.
An artist's creativity interacts with the visual medium.
That is a sufficient and necessary condition for art to exist.

Paint can only do what paint can do.
John Dewey (1958): A medium and artist's attempts to bend it to his will
Are the ingredients of art.
The visual medium means all art is visual so teaching art should be too.

A medium turns an artist's concepts into perceptual forms.
This indicates the various classes of art (and also crafts).
Music always deals with auditory forms (sounds) art with visual forms.
Literature is written language, dance with bodily movements, etc.

There is a manipulation of the media.
This may be (paint/canvas, keys/piano, words/paper).
Shows aspects of human behaviour other than or additional to creativity.
Action is usually multi-motivated, but studied and analyzed singularly.

Can you set up and do demonstrations?
Why do you want to do a demonstration?
Are you trying to make money?
Would you like to help people?
Have people asked you?
Perhaps you've done it before?

What exactly are you going to do?
Why will people want to see this demonstration?
Have you practiced sufficiently?

How long does it take?
Can the time taken vary?
Will you need to supply notes or other handouts?

How are you going to do it?
Who will want to attend?
How are you going to reach the people who should attend?
Have they seen something like your demonstration before?
What will attract them to your course?
Where will you find the people who would like your demonstration?

When will this happen?
What time of the year is best?
What day of the week and what time is best?

Where would be a good place?
Can you obtain such a place?
What (part of your) town, city, suburb, area would be best?
What exactly do you need?
Are you flexible?

Who will you need there?
Who will you need to help you?
Who will you need to contact about the demonstration?

Now what?
Sit down and think for a while.
Read these questions, as well as others that come to mind.
Write questions and answers to the questions (include your other ones).
See how they fit together.
Test your answers against your reasons for doing the demonstration.

Otherwise the whole idea is a waste of time.
You should plan a suitable demonstration and written it all down.
You might still need to shuffle ideas around so they are in a better order.

Read through it like someone attending your course.
Particularly the kind of person you want to attract.
Have you covered everything they'd want to know?
Double-check everything and then write it out in several different ways.
Did each different way will tend to suggest new ideas for you to use?

Is there another step?
Now plan a marketing campaign so people to come to your demonstration.
Who do you need to contact?
When is the best time?
How will you do it?
What is your background?
Why should artists come to your demonstration?
What can you do for them?

How much should you charge?
What will it cost you?
How much do you want to make?
How many people do you need there?
What is the most you can handle?
What is the least number you need to still make money?
What will it cost them (there may be costs above your charge)?

What should you earn if you do?
Demonstrations and workshops earn more for an organization.
Obviously there's more to do.
You need considerably more organizing skill than doing your own thing.
Demonstrations and workshops are similar.

Can you do it, best of luck, for it is fun and you can make money.
Use Powerpoint and telling, where needed.
Consider how, when, where, why, who and what of a demonstration?

4. The journey is the goal!

Life isn't reaching a destination, it's the way you go about things.
This doesn't mean what you do shouldn't have longer term implications.
You should be aware of these **BUT** focus on **DOING** things right.
Then the end looks after itself.
Focus on the present and continual improvement from that point.
But that improvement should be towards your goal.

So let's look at how you can focus on the journey!
There are some words that are critical guideposts for success.
For example one of them is 'convenient'.
To survive and thrive, a teaching business needs to be convenient.

Think of convenience and McDonalds and mega-businesses.
They didn't start that way.
By thinking 'convenience' they became convenient to their customers.

Take that word (convenient) and think about it.
Realize something about your own art teaching in relation to students?
Sit down, with a pen and paper.
Think of at least 3 ways that dealing with you could be more convenient.
That's what happened when McDonalds first started!

Focus on at least one idea per week in this way!

Were all those paintings that van Gogh did substandard?
They didn't sell whilst he was alive.
Have they changed since for now they bring astronomical prices?
But the paintings are still the same as the day they were done.

If they were "bad" in Vincent's day you'd think they are still "bad".
But what has changed is people's opinion rather than the works.
Opinion is something that astute marketing can and should influence.
That's one of the roles of marketing.

Instead of blaming your course for failure question the marketing.
Perhaps a failure to influence people's opinion in relation to your ability?
Possibly a failure to even find out what opinions were held to start with?
You get somewhere if you think about this weekly, particularly over time.

You can re-set your clients' buying criteria.
Let's have a look at this idea.
People come to most buying situations with flexible buying criteria.
You shop for a lawyer, accountant, mattress, or other items or services.
How specific is your 'decision-making' criteria?
Just how expert are you in those areas?
Probably not much of an expert at all!

Therein is an extraordinary opportunity.
Most people do **not** have a clue about most things they buy!
That applies to your classes too!

Potential students don't have highly sophisticated buying criteria.
They only know what they may have paid or received in the past.

So you can re-set the buying criteria for your entire market.
Make your classes their most logical choice.
At the same time provide the best financial result for you.
All this without changing what you teach!

An example in a different field shows the effect of buying criteria.
Domino's Pizza state 'we deliver pizza in 30 minutes or less or it is free'.
They still do.

Effectively this claim changed the buying criteria for pizza.
Delivery speed became the main criteria!
It's a change that earned the pizza franchise many millions of $$$ since.

What are 3 ways to change the buying criteria for your classes!

WHERE NEXT:

**BUT being a professional artist is NOW harder than it ever was.
These books are on earning money from a professional art career.**

Gallery Co-Operation
http://www.amazon.com/dp/B087637FFW

Selling Strategies
http://www.amazon.com/dp/B0882JH3WN

Copyright
http://www.amazon.com/dp/B0892HWYTV

Make Exhibitions Work
http://www.amazon.com/dp/B0882MFPGX

Art Hiring
http://www.amazon.com/dp/B0884JWR2S

Agents
http://www.amazon.com/dp/B08847Y9KS

Your Website
http://www.amazon.com/dp/B08846SWQP

Selling Prints
http://www.amazon.com/dp/B08846SWQW

Retirement
http://www.amazon.com/dp/B0884D9TBP

Art School
http://www.amazon.com/dp/B08849FV59

**BUT being a professional artist is NOW harder than it ever was.
This book is the last of a series on earning real money.
From a professional art career.**

TAKE THE PLUNGE and Consider a Gallery.
http://www.amazon.com/dp/B0874JF964
Hardback
http://www.amazon.com/dp/B09GQRB34T

NOT NOW:

Perhaps one of these books could interest you then?

Publish a book about your own memories.
YOU could publish them – like I did!
http://www.amazon.com/dp/B087DWKPTP

A simple way to start developing creativity.
If you are a parent, teacher or someone who meets a group regularly?
http://www.amazon.com/dp/B088T1KFQZ

This is the way most people start to become an artist!
http://www.amazon.com/dp/B088Y1DPL6

Some more of my memories.
http://www.amazon.com/dp/B088Y4RPL9